What People Are Saying about *Goodbye Hello Purpose*...

D1462406

Thank you so much for presenting a fresh alte. ....u *concept of the* mission statement! *This book is clear, concise, and obviously well thought out. Now, not only do I have a clear structure for defining purpose, but I also know how to apply it to running my organization.*
C. C. Stein
Director of Operations, Bid Daddy Auctions

A BRILLIANT book! I love it! I love the style. Easy reading. Great examples. Clear and concise. Makes me think I could do it . . . Good job!
Jean Block
Jean Block Consulting

I've never been in love with mission statements *but also know people need to have a shared idea of what the point is, so Cate's ideas about how to frame a purpose statement make so much sense. In fact, I'm trying to put her message to work right now with an organization I'm working with. The book is an enjoyable read; it is conversational, personal, practical, and understandable.*
Susan L. Pentecost
President, Magnus Consulting LLC

Cate's book gets right down to business, thereby setting the reader up for success—or at least quick and substantive results—that will sustain forward momentum and motivation and greatly increase the overall success of her readers. Much like Jim Collins' Good to Great, *this book has the potential to make a difference in both the personal and professional lives of all who read and apply its wisdom.*
Steve Cordova
Real Estate Entrepreneur, Cliffside Investments LLC

Energetic and motivating! It feels as though I've had a chat with Cate and have come away with a better understanding, fresh ideas, and the confidence to try these ideas out in my organization!
Tamara Spooner
Executive Director, NM Veterinarian Medical Association

As I was reading Cate's book, I saw how her notion of using purpose to organize and manage organizations could easily be applied to my law practice. In fact, it has been my attention to what Cate defines as the What *and the* How *that has kept me focused and consistent through several changes in the focus of my practice over the years. Now that her good advice is in book form, it will be a valued guide and reference going forward. It is well written and practical; I'll be recommending it to both business clients and colleagues.*

Gregory P. Turza, JD
Attorney and Counselor at Law
Law Offices of Gregory P. Turza, Park Ridge, Illinois

I loved this book! Clear, practical, personal. Cate clearly understands the challenges and frustrations of the workplace and, better, what to do about them. This book should be required reading for anyone who plans to work in an organization.

Jason Stein
Restaurant General Manager

After thirty-seven years of working for organizations (military, nonprofit, small business) and business coaching clients—none of whom have mission statements that had any connection whatsoever to their day-to-day operations—here come Cate's concept of purpose and her formula for articulating it so that it can be used as the foundation, framework, and guidance system for all organizational activities. For example, she simplifies decision making with one question: Is what we're considering congruent with our purpose? It's amazing to be walked through the process of defining purpose so that when you're finished, you (and everybody else) have a clear understanding of what to do, how to do it, and why. My new motto: I'm on purpose. Are you on purpose?

Guy Fleming
Guycoach: Your Business Coach for Life

Cate has written a smart and practical publication that moves beyond jargon and theory to powerful results. I finally feel I have the tools to move any department or organization from confusion to purpose.

Mark Livingston
Business Consultant

Goodbye
Mission Statement;
Hello Purpose

How to Harness Purpose as Your Most Powerful Management Tool

Cate Cardwell, MA

Charity Channel

PRESS

Goodbye Mission Statement; Hello Purpose: How to Harness Purpose as Your Most Powerful Management Tool

One of the **In the Trenches**™ series

Published by
CharityChannel Press, an imprint of CharityChannel LLC
30021 Tomas, Suite 300
Rancho Santa Margarita, CA 92688-2128 USA

charitychannel.com

ISBN Print Book: 978-1-938077-46-3 | ISBN eBook: 978-1-938077-34-0

Library of Congress Control Number: 2013939747

13 12 11 10 9 8 7 6 5 4 3 2 1

Printed in the United States of America

This and most CharityChannel Press books are available at special quantity discounts for bulk purchases for sales promotions, premiums, fundraising, or educational use. For information, contact CharityChannel Press, 30021 Tomas, Suite 300, Rancho Santa Margarita, CA 92688-2128 USA. +1 949-589-5938

Publisher's Acknowledgments

This book was produced by a team dedicated to excellence; please send your feedback to editors@charitychannel.com.

We first wish to acknowledge the tens of thousands of peers who call charitychannel.com their online professional home. Your enthusiastic support for the **In the Trenches**™ series is the wind in our sails.

Members of the team who produced this book include:

Editors

Acquisitions Editor: Linda Lysakowski

Comprehensive Editor: Kathy Jenkins

Copy Editor: Stephen Nill

Production

In the Trenches Series Design: Deborah Perdue

Layout Editor: Jill McLain

Administrative

CharityChannel LLC: Stephen C. Nill, CEO

Marketing and Public Relations: John Millen

About the Author

Cate Cardwell loves the premise of management. The expectation that a lone person would take on responsibility for corralling the talent, energy, and good will of even a single dynamic, unpredictable employee—one with unique abilities, interests, ambitions, motivators, and outside life—let alone *groups* of them, is quite the challenge! And she embraces this challenge with joy, humor, and practical solutions.

Thirty-some years of managing in a wide variety of industries has persuaded Cate that any organization can be set up so that it pretty much manages itself—not in spite of, but *because* of those unique employees. Further, she has observed how the setting-up process itself unites organizational members through common purpose and joint effort. The result is a workplace that stimulates, engages, satisfies, and uses its leaders and staff members well.

As head of her consulting firm, WonderOrganizations, Cate teaches clients how to become effective, confident, fearless managers. She envisions a world in which employed people everywhere wake up each day looking forward to going to work.

Cate has an MA in communication and organization development from Bowling Green State University.

Dedication

I dedicate this book to my daughter, Cecily, who believed in the value of this project from the beginning; willingly read unfinished chapters and listened to wild ideas at odd hours; generously indulged my occasional need for a reality check; cheerfully inserted the sidebars (!!); and most importantly, can always be trusted to say what she really thinks. Much love and many, many thanks.

Author's Acknowledgments

Heartfelt thanks to Jean Block, not only for making the introduction that led to the writing of this book, but also for her extraordinary generosity, support, advice, and friendship.

Much appreciation also to the CharityChannel Press editorial staff, who tirclessly examined each version of this manuscript—and did not stop until they had found, and suggested remedies for, every grammatical error, every formatting error, and every awkward sentence. Thank you!

Contents

Foreword xvii

Introduction. xix

Chapter One
Mission versus Vision versus Values versus Purpose 1

Chapter Two
Organizational Purpose: the Components 9

Chapter Three
Applying Organizational Purpose, Part One 23

Chapter Four
Applying Organizational Purpose, Part Two 37

Chapter Five
Applying Organizational Purpose, Part Three. 51

Chapter Six
Bringing It Home 63

Index 71

Summary of Chapters

Chapter One: Mission versus Vision versus Values versus Purpose.
The mission statement craze of the early 1990s generated two decades of misunderstanding and confusion by focusing on writing *statements* rather than defining *missions*.

Chapter Two: Organizational Purpose: the Components. Here is your step-by-step guide to defining, redefining, or tweaking your organization's purpose statement, followed by examples to show you how a well-crafted purpose can help you manage your organization and set you apart from everyone else.

Chapter Three: Applying Organizational Purpose, Part One. Ready for some detailed examples? This first one tells the story of an organization whose purpose doesn't mesh with its new external environment.

Chapter Four: Applying Organizational Purpose, Part Two. In our second detailed example, you'll observe how a department within a larger organization defined its own purpose, and then used that purpose to guide a sweeping, successful overhaul of itself. Oh, and inspired change in the rest of the organization, too.

Chapter Five: Applying Organizational Purpose, Part Three. Our final detailed example illustrates the ideal situation: prior to setting up a new organization, the founders define their purpose and then plan and design every facet of their operation in advance, based on their purpose.

Chapter Six: Bringing It Home. Saving the best for last. Learn step by step how you can apply the concepts and techniques discussed in this book to your own organization.

Foreword

I have come to know Cate Cardwell well over the last several years and respect both her professional skill and personal style. So when she asked me to be a peer reviewer for her new book, naturally I agreed. Well, I liked the book so much that I asked to write its Foreword, and here we are.

Cate puts a new spin on the notion of "mission" (prior concepts and definitions have plagued and confused organizational members for decades) by, first, offering a clear, straightforward, practical approach to articulating organizational purpose, and second, demonstrating how to use purpose to consistently, effectively, enjoyably manage organizations.

The examples Cate presents clarify the concepts and actions that she recommends, and the step-by-step instructions and suggestions are so detailed that organizational members at any level will be able to confidently begin experimenting with the concepts in their own organizations.

Part of why I'm so enthusiastic about this book is that its content reflects my own experience in organizations: For over two decades I have had positions of authority in a variety of organizations. The most successful of these have been the ones with a clear focus and mechanisms that lead them back to their intended purpose. For example, I am a longtime member of a volunteer organization that filters everything through the question: "Does this proposed action support our purpose, or not?" If it does, then we move forward. If not, then we revamp it or move on to something else. As a result, our daily operations are always consistent with our purpose. No confusion, no conflict.

I have also experienced the frustration of working in organizations that have mission statements, but whose day-to-day functioning is actually at odds with their missions. For instance, many sales organizations preach "customer first," but in reality, what is measured, rewarded, and talked about is dollars, not customer care.

Sadly, my experience in organizations has been mostly that their actions do not fit at all with their stated missions. This book has the potential to help all of us change that.

I hope that you will take the concepts and actions that are presented here and apply them to your own organizations. No matter what position you hold in your organization, I am confident that you will find something in this book that inspires you and helps you transform your organization into what you have always dreamed it would be.

Happy reading! Enjoy your journey!

Philip Conley
Financial Advisor
Waddell and Reed

Introduction

I remember the early 1990s when suddenly the topic of mission statements was thrust upon the consciousness of organizations in the United States. Regardless of industry, product/service orientation, or profit/nonprofit status, suddenly everybody was supposed to have a mission statement. And pretty much nobody did. Oh no!

Directors, presidents, and CEOs across the land began appointing committees to come up with mission statements for their organizations, and conference rooms everywhere resounded with abstract nouns, action verbs, and the secret sighs of committee members who wondered what they'd done to deserve such punishment.

In most cases, mission statements were eventually produced. They were either typed up nicely, placed in attractive frames and hung in reception areas, or put to rest in someone's drawer or filing cabinet. Pretty much across the board, the only value derived from these mission statements was that their organizations each now had one.

I was on one of those committees and can attest to the floundering and confusion that accompanied our efforts, beginning with the fact that none of us (we were all managers, positioned one to three layers below the top decision makers) had an inkling of what our organization's mission actually was. (Or if—gasp—there even was one!) After much discussion, we invited a senior manager to one of our meetings hoping for clarification, or at least a place to begin. What we learned was that he didn't have any better insight than we did. Daunted (but prohibited from resigning from this committee), we finally negotiated a mission statement for our organization. It was approved by someone at another location whom none of us had ever met, and the committee was disbanded. To our shared relief.

I could not reproduce that mission statement for you today if my life depended on it. How odd, you might be thinking, since I spent several months with colleagues toiling to get it just right . . . And it *is* odd. But it isn't surprising, given that

◆ none of us understood at the outset (or at the end either, now that I think about it) precisely what a mission statement was or how it was supposed to be used;

◆ although we committee members were all managers, we weren't privy to the thinking, planning, or decision making that took place at higher levels of the organization;

◆ as a result, we were crafting this mission statement in a vacuum;

◆ the statement we finally agreed on was thus essentially noncommittal (disguised in abstractions);

◆ our mission statement was never published or introduced to the rest of the organization;

◆ the fact that we now had a mission statement did not alter a single aspect of organizational life; and

◆ the mission statement that fulfilled our assignment was not in any way meaningful to me personally.

And that leads to why I'm writing this book.

I've worked with a variety of organizations over the past several decades and, without exception, I have encountered issues that, first, interfere with work getting done smoothly and effectively and, second, ruin the opportunities for satisfaction that exist in abundance in the workplace. These issues manifest in a host of persistent and irritating ways, which often misleads those in charge to suspect that any problem solved will automatically be replaced by another and, in extreme cases, that the situation is hopeless. Not so.

In fact, there generally is a single underlying problem, and it is this one problem that generates all the others. The problem is, simply, the absence of a sense of larger purpose that permeates the organization. This absence of purpose results in a lack of definition, framework, context, and direction in both organizational units and individual members.

So it is not surprising that we currently find legions of workers across the spectrum of organizations who don't know specifically what is expected of them, how exactly they're supposed to be doing their jobs, what constitutes successful performance and, finally, how what they do contributes to their organizations, their communities, the world. And this lack of clarity creates issues that interfere with work and ruin satisfaction in the workplace.

It doesn't have to be like that. And that's why I'm writing this book. My organizational adventures have convinced me that, despite external circumstances, any organization is capable of becoming a place of inspiration, challenge, collaboration, innovation, learning, achievement, and enjoyment for its members. To become that place, organizations need a purpose that is known and endorsed by everyone who works for them and that undergirds every aspect of everyday work life.

Unlike the approach I experienced on the mission statement committee so many years ago, where the goal was simply to develop a *statement* which was not connected in any way to organizational practice, in this book I will offer *mission* as a practical tool which, formulated, communicated, and lived properly, will drive every aspect of your organization's life. And the result will be a workplace filled with motivated, highly performing, involved, excited members who together continually strive for more and better—in accordance with your underlying purpose.

We'll begin with a discussion of terms—mission, vision, values, purpose. We'll sift through overlap and subtle differences and arrive at a workable definition of mission and an understanding of its essential components.

From there, we'll take a look at mission in action in an assortment of organizations, and finally, we'll explore fully how you can transform your organization's mission from simply a statement to the practical foundation of everything you do.

Let's begin.

Chapter One

Mission versus Vision versus Values versus Purpose

IN THIS CHAPTER

···→ How did the notion of organizational mission become so confusing?

···→ How can we approach mission so as to eliminate the confusion and focus on practicality?

···→ How do *vision* and *values* fit in?

I am a lover of context. Genuine understanding, I believe, depends on knowledge of background and setting. So, here's a brief history lesson:

Although organizations have been around since at least 3000 BC, it wasn't until the early 1900s that they became the objects of formal study. The discipline of Management was born, and its goals were (1) discovering the most efficient approaches to structuring, organizing, and managing organizations, and (2) advocating the universal application of those approaches in organizations.

Nonprofit organizations weren't initially included in formal organizational studies because at that time they were markedly different from the organizations that were capturing researchers' attention: for the most part, organizations that provided outreach and other charitable works were affiliated with/sponsored by larger religious organizations; they were staffed largely by volunteers; they dealt primarily in services rather than goods; and they represented only 1 percent of the economy. As a result, they weren't suitable places for studying the structural, organizational, or management issues that intrigued early researchers. (Some early charitable organizations that have been around for one hundred plus years have had a clear sense of mission from the beginning.)

Between the 1960s and early 2000s, nonprofits had grown to comprise around 9 percent of the US economy. Agencies without religious affiliations partnered with the government for scientific, defense-related, and medical research. Nonprofits with and without religious affiliation were running colleges, universities, hospitals, medical schools, professional associations, civil rights groups, gender rights groups, right-to-life groups, right-to-choice groups, homeless shelters, battered women's shelters, job-training programs, after-school programs, meals for the poor, food banks, think tanks, and on and on and on. As nonprofit organizations grew in size and budgets, they also grew in sophistication, hiring professionals to raise funds and manage their agencies and inviting high-ranking business professionals to sit on their boards.

Their leaders also began reading the same books and articles on effective organizational management that their counterparts in the for-profit sector were reading and began experimenting with the same approaches. For-profit and nonprofit organizations now had much in common: they faced very similar organizational issues, spoke the same organizational language, and had the same organizational management philosophies and techniques available to them.

Those philosophies and techniques have evolved over time as understandings of scientific analysis and human nature have deepened, as technological developments have advanced, as education levels of organizational workers have risen, and as each subsequent generation has perceived the world and its place in the world through different eyes.

What is most interesting and surprising to me about the evolution of management thought is the absence of even a mention of the universal need for organizational missions until the mid-1990s (excepting the one-hundred-plus-year-old charitable institutions mentioned earlier). Previously, the focus was limited to internal functions including planning, organizing, motivating, structuring, and performing tasks efficiently. No one talked about establishing the *framework* within which to plan, organize, manage, and produce. And no one suggested that organizational leaders regularly ask the most fundamental, practical, relevant questions for an organization to consider: Why are we here? What do we intend to do? How are we going to do it?

The Confusion Begins, Grows, and Persists

The bafflement surrounding organizational mission didn't arrive all at once; it became compounded in waves as mission *statements* took on lives of their own, separate from their organizations' *missions*, and definitions and interpretations of the mission *statement* were expanded and enhanced.

> *Mission.* This word has been appropriated by government, military, and business organizations to refer to their objectives and purposes. Its use was originally the exclusive province of religious missionaries as it described their outreach and conversion efforts as well as their bases of operation. In current (lengthy) dictionary definitions of *mission*, brief references to its organizational application appear (if at all) last.

Wave One

In the early to mid-1990s, books and articles propounding the absolute necessity for every organization to have a mission statement began appearing in journals and bookstores. And, since the notion of mission had been mostly absent both from theories about effectively managing organizations and from the organizations themselves, this sudden organizational requirement caused quite a stir. Unfortunately, the emphasis, as it was understood and acted upon by organizations, was on writing a statement, not on defining a mission. Hence variations of the mission-statement-writing scenario described in the Introduction played out in organizations all over the country, with similarly empty results.

In addition to the almost insurmountable difficulty of producing a mission statement in the absence of an actual mission, the organizational leaders responsible for strategic planning were rarely involved in the endeavor, which left mission statement developers struggling without benefit of the big picture. And, finally, the instructions on how to write a mission statement available in business/management books and articles gave confusing or conflicting information. As they still do today. Here are some examples:

◆ A mission statement answers the question, "What do we do?"

◆ A mission statement defines your primary customers, the products and services you provide, and the geographical area in which you operate.

◆ A mission statement is a snapshot of what your business is today.

◆ A mission statement is not about what you do; it's about the difference you make.

◆ A mission statement attracts investors/donors.

◆ A mission statement defines the organization's primary goals and objectives.

◆ A mission statement defines the organization's measures of success.

◆ A mission statement should be between thirty and sixty words.

◆ A mission statement should be short enough to fit on a business card or a T-shirt.

◆ A mission statement can be long or short.

◆ A mission statement inspires employees.

◆ A mission statement provides criteria for problem solving.

◆ A mission statement is memorable.

◆ A mission statement is as unique as your organization.

You get the idea.

Wave Two

Just as well-meaning organizational leaders and their staffs were recovering from the trauma of producing mission statements, along came the next directive from organizational experts: mission statements are not sufficient; everybody needs a vision statement, too.

Vision refers to the exercise of imagination, particularly regarding the ability to picture the future.

As teams of miserable middle managers struggled to sort out the differences between mission and vision statements so that they could—again in a vacuum—produce their vision statements, the confusion increased exponentially:

◆ A vision statement defines the way an organization will look in the future.

◆ A vision statement defines how the organization wants the world in which it operates to be in the future.

◆ A vision statement provides clear decision-making criteria.

◆ A vision statement has defined goals to be accomplished by a set date.

◆ A vision statement is a marketing tool.

◆ A vision statement inspires customers, employees, and investors/donors.

◆ A vision statement focuses on what is possible.

Values are traits, qualities, and characteristics that an organization (in this context) deems to be important. Values are the underpinnings for priority setting and decision making.

Wave Three

Just when statement developers thought it couldn't get any worse, a final edict was issued by organizational experts: mission and vision statements are important, but they aren't complete without a values statement.

◆ A values statement defines an organization's core beliefs.

◆ A values statement defines how an organization will value its customers, suppliers, and community.

◆ A values statement defines how people want to behave toward one another in the organization.

◆ A values statement defines traits or qualities considered important by the organization.

◆ A values statement communicates organizational goals and priorities to employees.

◆ A values statement represents the personal values of the majority of organizational members.

> *Purpose* explains why something exists; it is the reason for which something is created or done.
>
>

Eeeeeeaaaahhhhhh!

Looking Ahead

Given the evolution and contradictory guidelines surrounding the formulation of organizational mission statements, misunderstanding and confusion were inevitable. So let's make two changes:

First, let's replace "mission" with "purpose." As we've seen from the definition above, "mission" is traditionally—and formally, through its definitions—associated with religious, military, foreign-service, and other government-affiliated organizations and activities.

In contrast, "purpose" is associated with reasons (why something exists; why something was created) and with goals (what are we trying to accomplish?). None of its meanings even hint at religious, military, or other government affiliation, and in addition, "purpose" is unencumbered by association with the failed mission-statement "movement" briefly summarized above.

Second, let's stop focusing on *writing a statement*, and instead begin by *defining your purpose*. As we create, or develop, or reveal your organizational purpose, the statement that expresses it will pretty much write itself. And along the way, you will discover the powerful potential of a clear, articulated organizational purpose: it can provide the foundation and inspiration for your organization. And it can become your framework, your guidebook and, by far, your most practical management tool. To find out how, please read on.

To Recap

◆ Focus on organizational mission is a relatively recent development in management thought.

◆ Early attempts at defining organizational mission were generally frustrating and unsuccessful.

◆ There is often a striking difference between organizations' mission statements and their actual underlying purposes.

Chapter Two

Organizational Purpose: the Components

IN THIS CHAPTER

- ···➔ What elements are required to fully define your organization's purpose?

- ···➔ How can you use your organization's purpose to set you apart from other organizations in your industry?

- ···➔ How can your organization's purpose function as an effective management tool?

In order to formulate organizational purposes that help us manage our enterprises more effectively and with greater ease, we need to include several elements.

The *Why*

One of the difficulties the mission statement committees of old encountered was that while they were trying to create a statement that would sound good to potential directors, donors, investors, etc., they were neither connecting their statements to the reality of their organizations' day-to-day functioning nor adjusting their organizations' daily operations to reflect their statements.

To avoid that difficulty, I suggest that you ignore, for the moment, whatever has occurred in the past or is currently transpiring within your organization—and ask these fundamental questions:

◆ Why is this organization here?

◆ What is the reason for our existence?

◆ What gives meaning to our day-to-day activities?

The answers should reflect what you see as the end results of your organization's work: the contributions or improvements you make or intend to make in your clients' or customers' lives, in your community, or in the larger world. And when you focus on those larger, long-term contributions rather than your day-to-day activities, you and your organizational members will be able to find ongoing inspiration.

Whose Organizational Purpose Is This?

We are a global family with a proud heritage passionately committed to providing personal mobility for people around the world.

Answer: Ford Motor Company

On the other hand, organizations with purpose statements that express only their own ambitions—earnings, popularity, global status, number of outlets, or other internal success measures—miss the point.

While you are seeking the underlying reasons for your organization's existence, if you discover that you have either strayed from or never had a clear purpose, don't be concerned. This is the perfect time to define it or redefine it and adjust daily operations to reflect it. We'll talk about how to do this as we proceed.

And that brings us to the next element we need to include in a statement of organizational purpose.

The *What*

We've settled on our reason for existing. What comes next is defining the activities we are going to perform to bring our purpose to life.

Here are some examples:

The Golden Harvest Food Bank

The *Why:* "Our feeding program to the hungry sustains health, good nutrition, energy, human dignity and the opportunity for individuals to meet their full potential."

The *What:* "We provide food to six area agencies which collectively feed over one thousand meals per day to the hungry."

Virginia Sexual and Domestic Violence Action Alliance

The *Why:* "We are a coalition of people and agencies committed to ending sexual and domestic abuse."

The *What:* "We make sure your community has the resources it needs to respond effectively to sexual and domestic violence; we educate individuals, professionals, communities, and legislators on how to stop sexual and domestic violence from happening and how to help those who have been hurt by violence; we bring people together to build networks and to learn from each other in order to make Virginia safer."

Goodwill Industries

The *Why:* "Goodwill Industries International enhances the dignity and quality of life of individuals, families, and communities by eliminating barriers to opportunity and helping people in need reach their fullest potential through the power of work."

The *What:* "Goodwill Industries collects used household goods and clothing; trains and hires the unemployed or bereft to mend/repair them and to work in their stores; redistributes, donates, or sells the repaired products."

As these examples illustrate, *Whys* address the underlying reasons for the organization's existence: they specify organizational commitment to particular issues or the premises upon which organizations are founded, and they describe how the world will be bettered when they have fulfilled their purposes. *Whys* are theoretical, hopeful, inspiring. *Whats*, in contrast, outline the specific activities the organization will perform to fulfill their purposes. *Whats* are concrete and practical. We need them both if we want to define organizational purpose so that it becomes our prevailing guidance system.

What's Wrong with This Purpose Statement?

Since its inception in 1982, ABC has remained on the vanguard of political and community empowerment by developing influential leaders that strive to exert knowledge and power into its peers in order to attain mutual success. ABC is committed to academic excellence, leadership development, and cultural enlightenment, enhanced by a diverse cognizant membership. ABC strives to preserve and promote an inclusive intellectual environment for its members, in addition to the general community.

Answer: Lots of jargon, very little meaning.

A common misunderstanding that occurs during attempts to define purpose is mistaking *What* an organization does for *Why* it exists. To illustrate, let's posit a meals-delivery organization which, when asked why it exists, replies that its purpose is to deliver meals to the elderly. This is not actually the *Why* as we have defined it. Our *Why* would give us underlying reasons for delivering meals to the elderly such as: to improve the quality of life for our neighborhood seniors, or to ensure that seniors on a fixed income get enough to eat, or to provide nutritious meals to those who can't take proper care of themselves, or to end hunger in our city. You get the idea.

And now we come to the final element that we need to include in our statement of organizational purpose.

The *How*

The *How* incorporates values into the organizational purpose. This can be done in a variety of ways:

Many organizations develop values statements that consist simply of lists of values (integrity and respect are always included), but don't connect the values to behaviors, so it isn't possible to know how, or if, these values actually drive behavior in the workplace. For example, can we ever know what "honesty" means in an organization? Does it mean that no one takes home office supplies? That management tells its staff about the plan to move jobs overseas next year as soon as the plan is formulated? That production areas inform customers of the lower quality components they now use in their products? That organizational members don't lie—unless there's a compelling business reason to do so?

Some organizations create lists of their values and include how they operationalize them. In other words, they explain how their values are demonstrated in the workplace. This is a better approach than the simple list because it defines for stakeholders what each value means and how it is enacted in the organization. Goodwill Industries, example on the next page, does a good job with this.

Other organizations reveal their *Hows* by providing details of how they perform their *Whats*. Here's an example: *We generate electricity, deliver electricity and distribute natural gas* (the *Whats*) *in a safe, reliable, efficient, and environmentally sound manner* (the *Hows*).

Still other organizations include their *Hows* with their *Whys*. In the example, *To provide high-quality, compassionate, and comprehensive legal services to low-income persons*, "high-quality, compassionate, and comprehensive" are the *Hows*, and "To provide legal services" is the *Why*.

Finally, some organizations deal with the How internally, through procedures, policies, etc., rather than incorporating them in their statements of organizational purpose. For example, this policy (a How) reveals the organization's values regarding responsiveness to customers: "All phones will be answered by the second ring." And notice the values revealed by this policy: "Customer Service Representatives are expected to handle forty-five calls per hour," compared to the values embedded in this one: "Customer Service Representatives are expected to work with customers until the customers are completely satisfied." (Note: I have found, in general, that the actual values of an organization show up clearly in their employee handbooks.)

Each of these formats is fine; what really matters is that (1) all organizational members know of and endorse the values that underlie the performance of activities that are intended to fulfill their organization's purpose, and that (2) all activity occurring within the organization is directly related to its purpose.

Let's look at some examples, both good and could be better.

Goodwill Industries

Goodwill Industries International lists its values along with explanations of what those values mean within the organization. This provides a good framework for how organizational members act in the workplace:

Our Values

Respect—We treat all people with dignity and respect.

Stewardship—We honor our heritage by being socially, financially, and environmentally responsible.

Ethics—We strive to meet the highest ethical standards.

Learning—We challenge each other to strive for excellence and to continually learn.

Innovation—We embrace continuous improvement, bold creativity, and change.

Microsoft

In contrast, Microsoft's Values Statement is an example of the simple values list:

As a company, and as individuals, we value integrity, honesty, openness, personal excellence, constructive self-criticism, continual self-improvement, and mutual respect. We are committed to our customers and partners and have a passion for technology. We take on big challenges, and pride ourselves on seeing them through. We hold ourselves accountable to our customers, shareholders, partners, and employees by honoring our commitments, providing results, and striving for the highest quality.

It isn't clear from this statement how the values listed by Microsoft are enacted in its workplace. In this particular case, however, there is extensive information in the public record regarding Microsoft's behavior:

◆ Microsoft has paid over $1 billion in fines and restitution for illegally blocking competition in the United States.

◆ Microsoft was fined 499 million euros (US$666 million) in 2004 for violating the European Union's competition laws.

◆ Microsoft was fined an additional 899 million euros (US$1.35 billion) in 2008 for failing to comply with the EU's 2004 antitrust order.

◆ Microsoft was fined $32 million by South Korea for violating its competition laws.

◆ Microsoft has paid additional millions of dollars in settlements and fines resulting from lawsuits filed by dozens of private companies.

The lesson? Listing values is easy; choosing to have them guide behavior, not so much.

Another thing that strikes me about Microsoft's values statement is that it includes its employees in the list of external stakeholders (customers, shareholders, and partners). In other words, this statement makes Microsoft employees outsiders. Which begs the question: Who is the "we" in the values statement?

> **Whose Organizational Purpose Is This?**
>
> *To give ordinary folk the chance to buy the same thing as rich people.*
>
> Answer: Walmart

Starbucks

The original Starbucks included guiding principles with its mission statement. Please note that its *Why* addresses its own agenda rather than how it will contribute to the world, but its guiding principles do provide a semi-framework for decision making. Here are the mission statement and guiding principles of the original Starbucks:

> *To establish Starbucks as the premier purveyor of the finest coffee in the world while maintaining our uncompromising principles as we grow. The following six Guiding Principles will help us measure the appropriateness of our decisions: Provide a great work environment and treat each other with respect and dignity; embrace diversity as an essential component in the way we do business; apply the highest*

standards of excellence to the purchasing, roasting, and fresh delivery of our coffee; develop enthusiastically satisfied customers all of the time; contribute positively to our communities and our environment; and recognize that profitability is essential to our future success.

We want to create organizational purposes that function as powerful management tools; we can learn from the shortcomings of others and do better.

Why, What, How—Putting It Together

Unique *Whys* and *Hows* differentiate organizations operating in the same industries (i.e., performing essentially the same *Whats*) from one another. Let's see how it works.

Here are the purpose statements of three grocery stores that operate in the Chicago area:

Sunset Foods

Sunset Foods is a neighborhood supermarket dedicated to providing the finest customer service. We are small enough to get to know you and large enough to stock an outstanding selection of food, liquor, florals, and other items at competitive prices. Our friendly, competent staff works hard to make shopping at our store a pleasurable experience.

Jewel-Osco

Jewel-Osco is committed to serving its customers with the freshest and finest products and the most innovative retail features delivered by friendly, service-oriented associates. The company is equally committed to be a good citizen in every community in which it operates.

Each year, more than 6,000 organizations, which focus primarily on education, health, and hunger, receive support from Jewel-Osco in the form of volunteer hours, food donations, or monetary contributions. Of special note, Jewel-Osco is the largest single food donor to the Greater Chicago Food Depository, is a major supporter of the United Way, and is a founding member of the Chicago Minority Business Development Council.

Cub Food

> *Customers at Cub Food stores can save up to 40 percent on groceries without sacrificing quality. Small stores combined with the most frequently purchased grocery items generate significant cost savings for shoppers. Buying fewer products in tremendous volume gives us formidable buying leverage and enables Cub Food stores to offer products to consumers at dramatically lower prices.*

So what do we have? Three grocery stores with substantially different approaches to the grocery business, based on unique views of customer needs combined with their organizational values:

Sunset Foods, located in the pricey suburbs, is founded on establishing personal relationships with its "neighborhood" customers (it employed a full-time greeter in the early 1980s—long before anyone else); promising to "get to know you" and to make visits to Sunset "pleasurable" so customers want to return often; providing "an outstanding selection of food, liquor, and florals" so customers will make Sunset their go-to place for all their personal, family, and entertaining needs. The language selected for its statement of purpose evokes intimacy, quality, luxury, care, and pleasure, which sums up its values and reason for being. (Note: when Sunset Foods says "competitive prices," what it means is "at least twice what the item would cost elsewhere.")

Jewel-Osco was formed by the merger of a large grocery chain (Jewel) and a large pharmacy chain (Osco). The combination has made a greater number of goods and services available to customers.

I find the Jewel-Osco statement of purpose absolutely fascinating: in the first section, Jewel-Osco summarizes its grocery/pharmacy business in one sentence: ". . . committed to serving its customers with the freshest and finest products and the most innovative retail features delivered by friendly, service-oriented associates." This is followed by another sentence

What's Wrong with This Purpose Statement?

The mission of XYZ is to fight hunger through community partnerships.

Answer: Here we have sort of a *Why* and a tiny *How*, but nary a *What*.

which announces its commitment "to being a good citizen in every community in which it operates."

Its statement of purpose ends with a lengthy second section completely devoted to the details of Jewel-Osco's community involvement and service. It's almost as if the grocery-pharmacy business is a side line, and the real business is community service. Clearly, Jewel-Osco's heart belongs to community service. (Isn't this fun?)

Finally, we have Cub Foods. Again, the *Why* and the *How* are crystal clear: it runs no-frills grocery stores with limited products and low overhead and passes impressive savings on to their customers. So, if you choose to become a customer, do not expect service (you will navigate your cart down very crowded aisles, pack your own bags, and load your own vehicle), and do not expect to find your favorite brands (as stated in its purpose: Cub Foods buys fewer products in tremendous volume). But if you are financially strapped, you can save up to 40 percent on your grocery bill by making a few adjustments to your grocery shopping expectations and eating habits.

As a consumer, I like checking the purpose statements of organizations with which I am contemplating beginning a relationship. Naturally, I am drawn to those whose values are closest to mine because common values makes them suitable providers for me, and me a good client/customer for them. I have shopped at Sunset, Jewel-Osco, and Cub Foods and strongly prefer Jewel-Osco because (a) my needs for relationships were filled by friends and family and at Sunset, I felt that I was paying dearly for a relationship I didn't want; (b) while I love sales and bargains, the sacrifices required by Cub Foods due to the unavailability of desired products were greater than I was willing to make; and (c) Jewel-Osco offered extensive choices, good quality, and regular sales, and, frankly, I love their passion for community involvement.

Putting It Together, Part Two

Next, let's compare the statements of purpose of two homeless shelters, both located in Albuquerque, New Mexico.

Albuquerque Rescue Mission

> *The Albuquerque Rescue Mission exists to show the restoring love of Jesus to hopeless and homeless men, women, and children, resulting*

in spiritual and emotional healing and lifelong discipleship to Jesus. To do this we provide food, shelter, clothing, training, education, mentoring, and Biblical counsel.

The Program for Women: while living in this facility, up to ten women will be enrolled in a life restoration program designed to be completed in about twelve months. At the completion of the program, the goal is that the women will find employment, move to permanent housing, and lead productive lives.

The Program for Men: the New Life Program for Men is a holistic twelve- to eighteen-month program designed to help men who want to end the cycle of homelessness in their lives. The program addresses all areas in a man's life such as educational, vocational, physical addictions, spiritual needs, and barriers to residency and long term employment.

Metropolitan Homelessness Project's Albuquerque Opportunity Center

Metropolitan Homelessness Project's Albuquerque Opportunity Center's mission is to provide creative, innovative, and high-quality shelter and services for people experiencing homelessness in our community, while cooperating with neighbors and the broader community to end the injustice of homelessness.

MHP's Vision: Experiences of homelessness are rare, short lived, and nonrecurring.

MHP's Values: Respect and Dignity; Equity/Fairness; Justice/Compassion; Self-Determination.

I first want to point out that the Albuquerque Rescue Mission's organizational purpose is not fully revealed in its initial statement of purpose. To truly understand its Why and How, it is necessary to also visit the descriptions of its programs, because there we

Whose Organizational Purpose Is This?

To provide a global trading platform where practically anyone can trade practically anything.

Answer: eBay

find both another, central reason for the Albuquerque Rescue Mission's existence (". . . to end the cycle of homelessness in their lives") and further explanation of the How ("This life-changing program is intended to address the spiritual, educational, emotional, and physical needs of the participant").

So, what do we know about the Albuquerque Rescue Mission from reading its purpose statement and program descriptions? We know that, ultimately, it wants to end homelessness. We also know that it works with the chronically homeless, since it links "hopeless" with "homeless" and talks about ending the "cycle of homelessness" which it attributes to its residents. Finally, we know that Albuquerque Rescue Mission's twelve- to eighteen-month programs treat the whole person, and that Bible study, Biblical guidance, and establishing or reestablishing a relationship with Jesus are keys to the spiritual and emotional healing which it believes will ultimately end homelessness.

Metropolitan Homelessness Project's Albuquerque Opportunity Center also has as its purpose to end homelessness: "Our mission is to end homelessness in Albuquerque, on both individual and societal levels, through a unified voice of advocacy, prevention, and service."

Note: The above statement came from a one-page flyer. Its statement of purpose appears in greater or less detail on its website, welcome packet, miscellaneous flyers, letterhead, and donation cards. Since these variations all clearly share the *Whys*, the *Whats*, and the *Hows*, I feel comfortable mixing and matching them here. Again, what really matters is that (1) all organizational members know of and endorse the values that underlie the performance of activities that are intended to fulfill their organization's purpose, and that (2) all activity occurring within the organization is directly related to its purpose.

What is fascinating about this pair of homeless shelters is that they approach their shared purpose in completely different ways. As we have seen, the Albuquerque Rescue Mission provides twelve- to eighteen-month long programs that have Jesus and the Bible at their centers and address the emotional, physical, vocational, and spiritual needs of the chronically homeless.

In contrast, Metropolitan Homelessness Project is founded on research which indicates that only 3 to 5 percent of the entire homeless population is chronically homeless. The vast majority of homeless men and women are homeless only in the short term; hence MHP's Vision: "Experiences of homelessness are rare, short lived, and nonrecurring." Further, the research suggests that, on average, it takes this 95 to 97 percent of homeless people an average of thirty days to find employment and begin rebuilding their lives.

Guided by the research, MHP serves only adult males and is organized around a thirty-day stay limit. All MHP programs, policies, and expectations are designed to support residents' efforts at finding work and housing within thirty days. For example, the shelter does not open to residents until five p.m. daily, and residents must leave the property by six a.m., requiring them to fill their time during the day with activities other than hanging out at MHP.

In addition, each new resident meets with MHP's exit planner during his first week to discuss how he will use his time while at MHP and what he will do when his thirty days are up. The exit planner provides interested residents with free, personal voice mail so that they can contact and receive messages from prospective employers or family members, and explains how they can set up free email accounts. Having phone numbers and email addresses satisfies the requirement for contact information essential to applying for employment—without revealing the residents' current, and, for most of them, embarrassing state of homelessness.

> ### What's Wrong with This Purpose Statement?
>
> *TUV exists to do all the good we can, in all the ways we can, in all the places we can, at all the times we can, to all the people we can, as long as we ever can.*
>
> Answer: This is just silly. To be more precise, there's no *Why*, no *What*, and no *How*. This isn't a statement of purpose.
>
> **food for thought**

MHP also connects residents with volunteers who provide acupuncture, spiritual companionship, assistance with preparing resumes, interview prep, and job hunting strategy; provides discounted bus passes; has a small computer lab with internet access on site for the use of residents; and regularly hosts representatives of groups that provide medical assistance, mental health evaluations, and other life skills workshops. Residents who secure employment within their thirty days may apply for extensions so that they have additional time to live rent-free while they earn their security deposits and first month's rents.

According to volunteers who help residents with all aspects of their job searches, the majority of men who are interested in finding work have secured employment within the thirty days.

So far, we have laid groundwork, defined terms, discussed the elements vital to a working organizational purpose, assessed some organizational purpose examples, and seen how organizations in the same line of work can approach that work in markedly different ways because of their unique *Whys* and *Hows*. In our final example, the comparison between Albuquerque Rescue Mission and Metropolitan Homelessness Project, we began to see how an unambiguous organizational purpose can drive internal organizational management.

In the next chapter, we'll present the first detailed example of an organization using its statement of purpose to guide its setup and management.

Fasten your seat belts.

To Recap

◆ An effective organizational purpose comprises three essential elements.

◆ The purpose can be constructed in a variety of ways.

◆ A properly defined purpose distinguishes your organization from all the others.

Chapter Three

Applying Organizational Purpose, Part One

IN THIS CHAPTER

··→ What operational functions can be guided by a carefully formulated organizational purpose?

··→ What happens when an organization's purpose is no longer compatible with its external environment?

··→ What adjustments can be made?

I've been looking forward to this chapter because this is where we're going to finally begin seeing how we can use our organizational purposes to run all aspects of our organizations.

Over the next three chapters I'll present examples inspired by organizations with which I've worked in some capacity. The examples include for-profit, nonprofit, and nonprofit-but-sustained-by-a-social-enterprise-venture organizations. I have intentionally provided a range of organizational types to illustrate that the process we'll be exploring is effective regardless of for-profit/nonprofit/not-only-for-profit status. To preserve everybody's anonymity, the organizational names that appear in these examples have been invented.

The organizations you'll be reading about here are similar to most of the organizations that exist in the larger world: they either didn't have formal statements of purpose, or the statements of purpose they did have were incomplete, or perhaps they had fabulous statements of purpose but nobody knew about them. I'll point these situations out as we proceed, and you will see how we can reasonably fill in blanks, extrapolate purposes from our knowledge of the organizations, or even work pretty effectively with incomplete statements of purpose. Along the way, we'll discuss how to retrofit a purpose to an ongoing enterprise and how to adjust the operation of an ongoing concern to a new purpose.

I have intentionally included considerable detail, in hopes that (a) you will find some instances similar enough to your own experience that you'll be able to relate personally to the examples and that (b) when you witness the depth and pervasiveness of the issues that some organizations have overcome, you will feel confident that your own organization's problems can be resolved as well.

We'll begin each of our illustrations with background and purpose, then provide descriptions of staff and operations. After we've laid this groundwork, we will explore how we can apply organizational purpose to every aspect of organizational management. Please be aware that even though we define these aspects as though they are discrete, separate entities, in living organizations they are interdependent, overlapping, often untidy, and always non-stand-alone.

The organizational facets with which we'll be dealing, directly and indirectly, are

- ◆ structure
- ◆ workflow
- ◆ staffing
- ◆ performance management
- ◆ accountability, incentives, and rewards
- ◆ management/supervision
- ◆ communication
- ◆ planning

Structure refers to how an organization is set up. The components of organizational structure include reporting relationships, decision making responsibility, services, and physical layout.

Workflow entails selecting the programs, products, or services to be produced by the organization; defining the processes by which they are produced and delivered; specifying how work is distributed among staff members; determining what specific standardized procedures should be followed to complete each step of the process; and developing, then regularly updating, documentation of those procedures.

Staffing involves realistically defining employment needs; defining and implementing the hiring process, including recruiting/interviewing/extending offers; creating orientation and training programs for new, transferred, and promoted staff members; and tracking turnover/developing turnover prevention plans.

Whose Organizational Purpose Is This?

To bring inspiration and innovation to every athlete in the world.

Answer: Nike

Performance management programs in organizations are responsible for developing and administering performance standards and expectations; accurate, up-to-date job descriptions; performance measures; performance assessment/evaluation; and feedback, learning, and adjustment.

In the accountability, incentive, and rewards area, we grapple with how to inspire diversely motivated staff members to become more engaged and excited by what they are doing; how to hold them accountable for poor or marginal performance; and how to reward good performance without breaking the bank or inadvertently encouraging feelings of entitlement.

Management/supervision is concerned with defining management/supervisory effectiveness; preparing and/or training supervisory/management hopefuls for promotion; selecting criteria for promoting or hiring supervisory/management personnel; developing techniques for measuring and evaluating supervisory/management performance; and defining and imposing management/supervisory accountability.

Communication entails what gets communicated, why, when, to whom, and how it is disseminated throughout the organization.

> Note to all who manage or work in organizations: nowhere is there a prohibition against tweaking, adapting, clarifying, expanding, amending, or discarding and beginning anew to create our organizational purposes. They don't have to be perfect to be powerful. Plus, there is no time limit: it is never too late to get our purposes in order.
>
>

Planning comes in three basic flavors—short term, long range, and contingency—and encompasses deciding which of these types to develop, how to approach their development, and finally, what to do with the plans once they are developed.

Ideally, our organizations operate each of their facets in ways that are guided by, and in turn reflect and support, their organizational purposes: *Why* they exist, *What* they do, and *How* the things they do express their unique values.

Aliass Consulting

Aliass Consulting was started by three IT professionals on the East Coast. They had noticed a need among IT departments in their region for, first, expert teams to design, develop and implement large, complex IT systems and, then, for the teams (and their high salaries) to disappear. They also saw a great money-making opportunity. Thus Aliass Consulting was established to supply (for two- to four-year terms, generally) highly skilled IT teams to organizations that had big projects, but didn't want to hire permanent employees.

This venture took hold so easily and was so profitable on the East Coast that the partners eventually decided that one of them would relocate to the Midwest and open a branch office there. So Aliass Consulting VP Casey arrived in the Midwest armed with a business model rather than an organizational purpose—plenty of *What*, but no *Why* or *How*. She rented offices, began hiring staff, and called on clients. Casey quickly discovered that the IT climate in the Midwest was substantially different from that on the East Coast: salaries were proportionally higher, IT personnel universally were fielding eight to ten calls per day from headhunters and could change jobs in the blink of an eye, and IT departments were hesitant to outsource their huge IT development projects. As a result, Casey compromised the only element of an organizational purpose that she had—the *What We Do*—and began renting out her high-powered consultants as contract employees. Her focus was profit, and if she stopped to think about the impact her abrupt step-away from the foundational business plan would have on her staff or her clients, it didn't influence her decision.

With Casey's new approach, Midwest Aliass Consulting grew rapidly, expanding from thirteen to sixty-eight consultants in just over two years. Aliass Consulting's IT professionals all had college degrees and ate-slept-breathed IT. They were professionally ambitious to a remarkable extent, and they expected acknowledgment and appreciation of their skills and achievements at regular intervals. They also expected their managers to be as interested as they were in their future prospects with Aliass Consulting: career path and training opportunities, promotion possibilities, and, naturally, when they were going to get those juicy assignments they'd been promised.

When the original consultants were hired, they had unlimited access to their leaders, everybody knew everybody and everything that was going on within Aliass Consulting and between Aliass Consulting and its clients, and excitement permeated the organization. Now, the old-timers were unhappy because that "family feeling" had disappeared, there was no longer an inner circle for them, and they felt left out. Plus, come to think of it, the work wasn't very stimulating.

The newer hires were unhappy, too, because while they'd been promised prestigious consulting jobs, most found themselves deposited at client sites doing mundane maintenance work, essentially functioning as temporary

---

What's Wrong with This Purpose Statement?

LMN's mission is to improve the effectiveness of the nonprofit sector by providing information technology solutions that facilitate and enhance communication and engagement between nonprofit organizations and their stakeholders. We do this by offering software tools and services, training, and consulting that help nonprofit organizations raise funds and communicate with their stakeholders online, and manage their operations more effectively.

Answer: Another case of jargon interfering with the message, but we do have a *What* and a *How*. No *Why*.

food for thought

employees. Managers from the home base would show up at their accounts occasionally, but they were there to talk with the clients about additional work, not to offer support to their seething consultants.

The result of all this consultant unhappiness was turnover. Lots and lots of turnover. And the result of all this turnover was eroded client confidence and satisfaction. The result of the client dissatisfaction was a marked decrease in revenue. And that's when company leaders decided something needed to be done.

Adjustments

They began by sending a trusted intermediary to meet with all the consultants, individually at first, and later in groups of eight to ten. The consultants' complaints, requests, and suggestions spurred many frank discussions in the office about what to do and how to proceed. Ultimately, an important decision was made: Aliass Consulting would begin paying more attention to its consulting staff. This decision resulted in the production of a formal Technical Management Plan, which laid out Aliass Consulting's philosophy (statement of purpose) and how the philosophy was to be implemented. The plan was distributed to all organizational members and announced at the annual organizational meeting that year.

The following was Aliass Consulting's new statement of purpose:

> *Aliass Consulting is founded on the commitment to deliver superior technical services to its clients. To do so requires that we hire quality technicians, that we build quality support systems in the areas of marketing, recruiting, and administration, and that we design an effective management structure to ensure growth and profitability, and oversee delivery of high quality technical product.*

You'll notice that this purpose statement consists only of Aliass Consulting's *What*, and that the *What* has shifted from sending elite IT teams to design, develop, and implement large IT systems for clients, to "deliver[ing] superior technical services to its clients." This new language allows for either elite teams or temp employees, a significant departure from East Coast Aliass Consulting's *modus operandi* and from the recruiting promises made to Midwest Aliass Consulting's IT professionals.

This next excerpt illustrates how Aliass Consulting used its purpose statement to redefine its structure:

As our branches grow, this management structure evolves to accommodate larger numbers of both technicians and accounts. At the outset, we have one senior manager who, from the Aliass Consulting office, oversees the entire technical staff. As the staff grows, it becomes clear that one manager cannot adequately cover all these responsibilities. We realize, too, that many of our client and technical staff problems cannot be solved, or perhaps even understood, from the distance of the office. Our technical management should be on the site where we are doing our marketing and fulfilling our contractual commitment . . .

> ## Whose Organizational Purpose Is This?
>
> Our vision is to be earth's most customer-centric company; to build a place where people can come to find and discover anything they might want to buy online.
>
> Answer: Amazon.com

Aliass Consulting's Technical Management Plan is the philosophy of management of Aliass Consulting's technical field staff which is distinguished by the assignment of administration, personnel, and technical management responsibilities to many key senior personnel who are in the field. It is summarized as follows:

Aliass Consulting's business is in the field and its management should be decentralized at the field level.

The marketing, administration, and technical office staff exist to support the field management structure.

The Technical Management Plan included specific procedures for adapting organizational structure as staff size increased:

Aliass Consulting is designed to adapt to the changing needs of clients and staff as each Aliass Consulting branch develops from a small to a midsize to a large operation. At the outset, all technical matters are overseen by a Technical Manager, who is also responsible for administration and personnel management, marketing, and recruiting support.

As the technical staff grows to forty to fifty consultants, the Technical Manager's responsibilities are taken over by four to six Account Liaisons, senior technicians in the field selected to manage Aliass Consulting's activities at their particular accounts. They report to a Regional Technical Director who, relieved of the day-to-day management of all accounts, concentrates his efforts on business planning and quality control.

As the technical staff approaches sixty . . .

You get the idea.

In response to a downturn in business and the hostility emanating from its technical staff, Aliass Consulting recognized the need to better support its consulting staff. As a result, it developed and articulated a Technical Management Philosophy that presented its purpose (still an incomplete purpose, yet capable of providing some important guidance nonetheless) and announced its intentions toward its clients. At the beginning of the ten-page document, Aliass Consulting redefined its structure to enable "providing superior technical services to clients." It laid out a very specific formula for structuring Midwest Aliass Consulting and future branches in a way that ensured on-site access to Aliass Consulting's supervisors for all consultants working in the field.

Further Adjustments

For technical staff working at client sites, the Technical Management Plan left some things to be desired. First, the "senior technicians in the field selected to manage Aliass Consulting's activities at their particular accounts" as described in the Technical Management Plan, in practice, performed technical work alongside the other consultants at client sites. Ultimately they were as isolated and uninformed about what projects were being generated by the home office as anybody else. Their only real supervisory function was to make sure that consultants turned in their time sheets on time. Secondly, the ongoing lack of management (their on-site "managers" didn't count) appreciation for the talent and efforts of their consultants led to even lower morale in the field and more turnover among technical staff.

In an effort to provide the consulting staff members with more of the feedback they kept requesting, Aliass Consulting next decided to revise its performance review procedures. The regional director sat down and laid out his goals for the new performance review system:

◆ It should help minimize and control turnover.

◆ It should be an educational vehicle for instilling reasonable salary expectations.

◆ It should function as a personal development tool, a career planning tool, and an outplacement tool.

◆ It should act as an Aliass Consulting internal relations tool, reinforcing the strength of the organization.

◆ It should provide a mechanism for collecting feedback on Aliass Consulting's performance from client accounts.

◆ It should help counteract the remoteness of the consulting environment.

You may have noticed that five of these six goals were designed to meet Aliass Consulting's needs, and that "Providing the consulting staff with feedback on their performance" as a goal for the new performance review system didn't even make the list. You may also recall that disregard for the effects of Aliass Consulting's decisions on its consulting staff had created serious problems in its short past.

This time, however, the goals were discussed at length among organizational leaders, and they agreed that no single performance review system could reasonably be expected to accomplish all the above. Eventually, they approved a five-part Staff Support Services program which would not only meet Aliass Consulting's goals, but

---

What's Wrong with This Purpose Statement?

To advance the common good by leading, strengthening, and mobilizing the independent sector.

Answer: What is the "common good?" And who is the "independent sector?" If statements of purpose cannot be clearly understood, they aren't useful.

food for thought

was designed to meet the needs of the technical staff as well. This program represented a major turning point for Aliass Consulting in that, first, each phase of the program had its own clearly stated purpose, including the *Why*, the *What*, and the *How*, and, next, the program was centered around creating satisfying, successful experiences at Aliass Consulting for its consultants.

Staff Support Services included:

Part One: Orientation for New Hires

The Why: *The goals of a more comprehensive orientation are to (a) equip new hires with the information they need to be effective in the field and (b) impart a sense of Aliass Consulting identity.*

The agenda will make Aliass Consulting's expectations of new consultants and the various facets of their jobs very clear. Providing them with an understanding of the consulting business and of their parts in it will prevent misunderstanding and misconception in the field.

The What: *Main topics to be covered will be: the nature of consulting; our marketing procedures; how we get business; what specifically are the contributions of technical consultants to Aliass Consulting and their roles with respect to clients; grievance procedures; performance appraisal.*

The How: *Previously: There is not a central person coordinating and following through with the scheduling, so that the schedule new hires receive for orientation is rarely the schedule followed. Sometimes days go by. This disrupts the assimilation of the new hire into Aliass Consulting and makes us look disorganized. We are also left with very little idea of who has been told what.*

New Plan: Meeting between the new employee(s) and an HR rep is the first item on the orientation agenda. After this

---

Whose Organizational Purpose Is This?

To give unlimited opportunity to women.

Answer: Mary Kay Cosmetics

presentation, we will proceed with the other introductions [includes four functional area managers based in the office]. We will explain that the new hires will also meet with a Marketing Rep and our Regional Director at some point during the first week.

Previously: The emphasis of a great deal of our current orientation is the Aliass Consulting organization: Aliass Consulting systems, Aliass Consulting procedures, Aliass Consulting regulations.

New Plan: We need to design part of our orientation around new employees so that they are drawn in and made to feel part of the larger organization.

Part Two: Regular Staff Meetings

The Why: The purpose of staff meetings is to promote a sense of unity and company identity, and offset whatever isolation or dissatisfaction may be experienced at a client account.

The What: Involve each consultant in a bimonthly meeting facilitated by an HR rep. To accomplish this, a group of eight to ten consultants will meet each week at eight a.m., in the office over breakfast provided by Aliass Consulting. No management will be present.

The How: Each agenda will include: Aliass Consulting news; ongoing instruction; forum for questions, complaints, and suggestions.

Part Three: Revised Performance Appraisal

The Why: The objective of our review system is to ascertain what an individual's performance has been over a specific period of time, and under what circumstances. The ultimate goal is increased effectiveness on the job.

The What: All technicians will be reviewed upon completion of each assignment (or at the six-month point for long term projects). Each review will be structured as a dialogue between supervisor and employee. In the process, we will receive a review of Aliass Consulting by the employee.

The How: All results are treated equally. We are as interested in assessing the factors that contribute to success—so that we can duplicate them—as we are in assessing the factors that contribute to failure—so that we can learn to avoid them.

Part Four: Career Counseling/Annual Salary Review

The Why: *Salary review combined with career counseling can be used effectively as a turnover deterrent. A staff of people with clearly defined goals and plans is a stable, predictable staff.*

The What: *Salary will continue to be reviewed annually, with performance appraisals from the year forming the basis for salary increases. The in-depth career counseling will include both long- and short-term goal setting, projection of future needs, and a determination of where Aliass Consulting fits with respect to those needs and for how long.*

The How: *Both management and technical career paths are defined so that opportunities for growth and advancement exist for all technicians.*

Part Five: Exit Interviews

The Why: *An exit interview gives us the opportunity to carefully examine the employee's reasons for leaving so that we can discover and correct problems within our organization, if they exist, and avoid further turnover.*

The What: *The interviews will be conducted at the office by the HR representative.*

The How: *We are interested in hearing employees' assessments of their experiences with Aliass Consulting as well as their reasons for leaving. We will respond with a statement regarding their contributions to Aliass Consulting over the period of employment.*

Lessons Learned

When we first met Aliass Consulting, Vice President Casey had just arrived in the Midwest to open its first branch office. Her plan was to implement the Aliass Consulting business plan which had been so successful on the East Coast. It became clear in short order, however, that what had worked in the East wasn't so well suited to the Midwest. Casey then revised the plan to assure contracts with clients and revenue streams.

The results were mixed: Casey got her accounts and revenue, but when she changed direction regarding the type of work Aliass Consulting did, she broke the hiring promises she had made to her consultants. They began leaving Aliass Consulting two and three at a time, leaving Aliass Consulting's client accounts short staffed, and jeopardizing the revenue-generating relationships Casey had established.

At that point, Casey invited her management staff to participate in discussions about what to do next, and those conversations led to the decision to solicit input from Aliass Consulting's technical staff, a first for the organization.

Relatively quickly, input from Aliass Consulting's managers, consultants, and clients yielded a new approach to the business: the primary focus was still on making money, but the business plan (Aliass Consulting's *What*) expanded from its original commitment to expert teams and big IT systems to include temporary, short-, and long-term contract assignments. As a result, the organization altered its recruiting process to include midlevel IT professionals in addition to the experts who had been their only hiring target previously.

> ## What's Wrong with This Purpose Statement?
>
> *The QRS Institute advances the power of individuals to take informed and compassionate action to improve the environment of all living things.*
>
> Answer: There's no *Why*, a vague and very unrealistic *What*, and no *How*.
>
> ## food for thought

More significantly, Aliass Consulting realized that it could produce even more revenue by using its technical staff to generate ideas and solve problems for the organization, in addition to their work in the field. And so Aliass Consulting added a *How* (the values piece) to its business plan (organizational purpose).

This additional piece elevated consultants to participating members of the organization through a five-step staff support program that guided staffing, performance management, accountability, and communication.

Grumbling at accounts stopped, and turnover dropped from 32 percent to 4.2 percent.

What we can learn from Aliass Consulting is that our organizations and our staff members are flexible. We can get off track or change our directions without fully anticipating the negative results that may ensue, but we can always reassess and make revisions. And when we get it right—right for our goals, our staffs, and our clients—we can succeed. Wildly.

Next up, the story of a department within a unit, within a larger nonprofit publishing company. Read on.

To Recap

◆ Organizational purpose can be used to guide all facets of its operations.

◆ An organization's purpose doesn't have to be perfect (or complete) to be powerful.

◆ It's never too late to tweak, adjust, expand, clarify, or replace your organization's purpose.

Chapter Four

Applying Organizational Purpose, Part Two

IN THIS CHAPTER

---→ What happens when there is no purpose guiding organizational activities and decision making?

---→ What options are available to departments, teams, and individuals?

---→ Where can we begin, and how do we proceed?

Our next *organizational purpose as management tool* adventure comes from a nonprofit publisher of books and periodicals called Aliass Publishing. Specifically, the action takes place in the publisher's subscription fulfillment unit.

The subscription fulfillment unit of Aliass Publishing consisted of the following functional areas:

First was the Call Center, which had responsibility for answering subscriber calls, providing customer service, taking orders, and updating accounts.

There were two product areas, Books and Periodicals. They generated requirements for developing computer programs (jobs) that allowed them to set subscriber rates, handle billing, collect payments, record payment histories, and an assortment of other subscriber-related functions.

The programming areas wrote the needed jobs and turned them over to Production Control, the department responsible for scheduling and running the jobs and then distributing reports.

The operations area allocated appropriate hardware to run each job, and other service areas within the data center (microfiche, video, print) processed and distributed outputs such as mailing labels.

Finally, the warehouse area affixed mailing labels to all book and periodical orders and shipped them to their subscribers.

Production Control: Rude Surprises

This is the story of Production Control, a small department within the subscription fulfillment unit. I have chosen to include it because it illustrates quite nicely that if you are working in an organization that doesn't have a statement of purpose driving its activities and uniting its staff members, you don't have to feel limited or directionless. Instead, you can create a purpose for your unit, or department, or work team, or even just for yourself, that ties in to the *What* of your larger organization, but adds the *Why* and the *How*. This purpose can then be used to guide your group and personal activities and decision making, and good things will result—at the very least, for you, and at most, for your larger organization.

Whose Organizational Purpose Is This?

Use our pioneering spirit to responsibly deliver energy to the world.

Answer: ConocoPhillips

Here's how it unfolded at Aliass Publishing.

The Production Control Department was part of the unit's data center. It was a three-shift, six-day/week, thirty-two-member operation responsible for scheduling, submitting, monitoring, and seeing through to successful completion all programming jobs for the Books and Periodicals areas. The department distributed outputs and performed a variety of other user support functions as well.

Our tale begins with the arrival in Production Control of Dana, the new department manager. As he entered the department for the first time, he saw a sea of desks with drawer pulls and legs missing, computer printouts piled everywhere, staff members wearing sweatshirts and jeans rushing back and forth across the department, phones ringing constantly, and messages written on scraps of paper scattered everywhere. There was no office for Dana; he was referred to a desk behind all the others (the only desk with a single drawer that locked), from which vantage point it was assumed that he would keep an eye on everyone. At least that is what his predecessor had done.

As Dana got to know production control's staff and users and learned about the department's work, he discovered serious problems in five areas:

◆ department functions

◆ space issues

◆ staff

◆ incoming-work standards

◆ department performance standards

Department functions consisted of an incompatible mix of sophisticated technical work and repetitive clerical detail, and all staff members were expected to perform all functions. The staff members who enjoyed technical work didn't have much patience for clerical detail, and the staff members who excelled at clerical detail were generally not particularly adept at the technical work.

In addition, Production Control had long been a dumping ground for the product areas in that whatever functions users found inconvenient, they had diverted to Production Control. No one in the department had ever refused the extra work and, as a result, Production Control performed dozens of tasks that had previously been done elsewhere in the unit.

Consequently, Production Control had no clear cut, defined set of responsibilities. Expectations varied by user and many of these expectations were unspoken. From the users' perspective, Production Control perpetually failed to carry out its responsibilities; from Production Control's perspective, its staff worked hard and competently to satisfy users that refused to be satisfied. The department felt helpless and victimized.

What's Wrong with This Purpose Statement?

The Center's mission quickly grew to include consulting work with jurisdictions across the country and the world. The Center has received numerous awards for its efforts, including an Innovations in American Government Award from Harvard University and the Ford Foundation, and the Prize for Public Sector Innovation from the Citizens Budget Commission.

Answer: This is a promotional piece, not a statement of purpose.

food for thought

Space issues were evident in the crowded desks, inadequate printout storage area, and lack of an office in the department. Because there was no office, Dana had to wait for a conference room on another floor to become available whenever he wanted to deliver a performance appraisal. Staff correction either waited for an available conference room or was conducted in hallways or in whispers within the department itself. There were no secrets in Production Control, and the lack of privacy was a strain on everyone.

Staff difficulties abounded. Production Control serviced the two product areas, Books and Periodicals. On first shift there were two supervisors, one for Books, and the other for Periodicals. They worked at adjacent desks and all they had in common was dislike for one another. Each had a specialized staff; there was no cross training. Second and third shifts were smaller, and everybody could process work from both product areas.

In addition to the supervisors, there were two "liaisons" on first shift who were senior staff members with responsibilities that were mysterious and lay outside of production control's purview.

Not surprisingly, there was no secretarial support in Production Control. Dana was told to use a secretary located on a different floor, but this was so inconvenient and time consuming that he ended up typing all his own work.

As if there weren't already enough tension in the department, each of Production Control's three shifts believed that the other two shifts were lazy and incompetent and felt free to discuss these beliefs loudly, among themselves and with users.

When it came to *incoming-work standards*, there weren't any. The department was responsible for around three hundred regularly scheduled production jobs and any number of one-shot jobs. Each job had unique setup, submission, and write-off procedures, which meant that all of the department's work consisted of exception processing. The consequences of this were that training took forever (staff had to learn each job rather than standard setup, submission, and write-off procedures), and the potential for error was enormous.

To make matters worse, almost every job required some sort of manual intervention during the submission process. Again, there was tremendous variation in the type of intervention and the point at which it was required. More opportunity for error.

There was no documentation for most of the jobs, and the documentation that did exist was obsolete due to frequent programming changes.

Finally, although Production Control was charged with submission responsibility for all production jobs, it was not uncommon for programmers to submit jobs from their own computer terminals. However, because the jobs were classified as production, they would then be automatically routed to Production Control's printer and suddenly appear in the department. This caused considerable confusion since these jobs weren't on the department schedule, and the investigation demanded by such incidents wasted substantial time.

Department performance standards were also sorely lacking. Because each job required unique handling, no one had been able to figure out how to quantify performance expectations or results. For example, one staff member could write off ten jobs in an hour while another staff member would write off only two jobs, and yet the person writing off two jobs was the more productive.

Clearly, with such chaos in the department, there was work to do.

Production Control: Department Purpose and Its Application

The very first thing Dana, his supervisors, and liaisons did was create a statement of purpose for the department:

[The Why:*] Production Control ensures that Aliass Publishing's subscribers receive their books, periodicals, and invoices on time and that their order/payment histories with Aliass Publishing are complete and up to date, [the* What:*] by scheduling, submitting, and overseeing successful completion of all batch production jobs, [the How:] with continuously improving accuracy, smoothness, and efficiency.*

Then they compared Production Control's day-to-day operations with its new purpose and found three major obstacles to "continuously improving accuracy, smoothness, and efficiency." These were (1) the staff; (2) the work; and (3) the entire setup. Production Control's transformation was going to take some time.

There were two projects of the highest priority, and everyone in the department participated in both. The first was getting a handle on the department's actual performance. Production Control as a department was generally assumed to be incompetent by the rest of the subscription fulfillment unit. While the public critiques of Production Control staff by other Production Control staff contributed to this impression, it was mainly due to the large number of errors that occurred during the running of jobs. No one, in fact, knew how many errors were committed, and it was clear that many of the problems that caused jobs to abort, thus requiring expensive reruns, were the result of programming and computer operations errors. So what was really going on?

Whose Organizational Purpose Is This?

We inspire and nurture the human spirit—one person, one cup, and one neighborhood at a time.

Answer: Starbucks

First, they developed a problem reporting system that consisted of an individual report for every production problem. Each report included a brief description of the problem; explanation of the action taken to resolve the problem; results of the action taken; name of the Production Control staff member who did the work; and, finally, the cause of the problem. The choices were: Production Control error, programming problem, hardware failure. All reports were copied and distributed daily to the computer operations area and the appropriate user and programming groups.

The problem reporting system was the first mechanism Production Control had ever had for measuring its own performance. It revealed the percent of production problems caused by department staff, which indicated training needs and provided a base for goal setting.

Next, the department began tracking rerun rates by job, by product area, and by cause of problem. Staff members developed graphs to illustrate these rates and the changes over time and published them. The entire Production Control department watched with satisfaction as its rerun rate decreased from 6.7 percent initially to consistently less than 1.5 percent. At the same time, Production Control's reputation improved substantially throughout the unit as users saw that, in fact, Production Control was responsible for only a fraction of the production problems.

The second highest priority project was unifying the Production Control staff. Clearly, the words "smoothly" and "efficiently" didn't apply to a department comprised of staff members who didn't trust or respect their fellow members.

Dana began this project by initiating a monthly meeting that all shift supervisors and liaisons were required to attend. Each agenda included a problem for them to solve, and the senior team learned to work together to create solutions. Their resulting new attitudes of respect toward each other and the staff on the other shifts spread to their subordinates, and the departmental tension began to subside.

The next project was determining which staff members were productive and which were not. Supervisors were persuaded to take a more active role in assigning work and monitoring its completion. Eventually, they knew precisely what everyone was doing and had some genuine basis for evaluating their subordinates' work. The nonproductive left the department, for the most part of their own accord. Morale and performance improved.

Cross training on first shift followed: one Book person and one Periodicals person traded places each month until they were all cross trained. Finally, first shift was consolidated under one supervisor.

Having dispelled the tensions between shifts and developed and implemented performance measures for the department, it was time to deal with the nature of Production Control's work. The ultimate goal was to formally reorganize the department, creating a Production Support group to perform technical functions and a User Support group responsible for the clerical work and relocated to the computer center, but there was still a lot of preparation to be done before the department would be ready.

The Adventure Continues

For Production Control to really be able to ". . . schedule, submit, and oversee successful completion of all batch production jobs with continuously improving accuracy, smoothness, and efficiency," it was essential to replace all the exception processing with standardized procedures. Automating manual processes appeared to be the most efficient and effective approach to standardizing Production Control's work, so two systems analysts were added to the department. They brainstormed innovations together with the leadership team, and then the analysts refined or expanded on the ideas, developed plans for execution, and implemented the fixes.

The procedure-standardizing projects included:

◆ Putting reports to tape rather than printout so they would be printed and distributed by the computer printing department rather than by Production Control. This eliminated the bulk of the department's printout processing and storage problems.

◆ Generating a standard transmittal sheet at the end of each job that contained write-off instructions and routing information. This move eliminated the production, storage, and use of over two hundred separate forms.

◆ Eliminating the need for manual intervention at the time of submission by having dates automatically supplied by the system, by using the data center's computer tape retrieval system to supply tape numbers, and a dozen other clever things. These changes greatly reduced and, in some cases, eliminated the chance of submission error and resulting costs of reruns.

◆ Automatically scheduling and submitting jobs. Production Control staff researched, secured authorization to purchase, and began implementing an automated scheduling software package. This move eliminated the possibility of overlooking jobs on the schedule or running jobs out of sequence.

What's Wrong with This Purpose Statement?

The mission of FGH is to educate and empower families affected by autism and other neurological disorders, while advocating on behalf of those who cannot fight for their own rights. We will educate society that autism is not a lifelong incurable genetic disorder but one that is biomedically definable and treatable. We will raise public and professional awareness of environmental toxins as causative factors in neurological damage that often results in an autism or related diagnosis. We will encourage those in the autism community to never give up in their search to help their loved ones reach their full potential, funding efforts toward this end through appropriate research for finding a cure for the neurological damage from which so many affected by autism suffer.

Answer: A statement of purpose is not the place to describe every activity in which an organization engages. This example is far too long; very heavy on the *Whats*, no *Why*.

food for thought

Each project that Production Control wanted to undertake to make its performance "more accurate, smoother, and more efficient" had to be cleared with product and programming areas and with computer operations if they were involved. Production Control teams were in a constant state of negotiation, but each success took them closer to fulfilling their purpose.

As a complement to all of the projects that were moving forward, Production Control's scope of responsibility was redefined, and then the product areas were persuaded to reabsorb their own work. The department's scope of responsibility proclamation was published unit-wide to prevent any future misunderstandings regarding what activities Production Control would and would not perform.

At this point, the supervisors separated clerical functions from technical functions within the department to determine who was best suited for each type of work. Taking the first step toward the restructuring while Production Control was all one department had several advantages. First, it gave everyone time to adjust. Secondly, it gave staff members the opportunity to revise their definitions of clerical and technical functions as they discovered some gray areas once they began. Last, they were able to ascertain the level of interdependence between the two groups and determine what changes needed to be made for them to operate independently and from different locations. Most staff members were relieved to be assigned to the work they performed the best and enjoyed the most.

> ### Whose Organizational Purpose Is This?
>
> *We organize the world's information and make it universally accessible and useful.*
>
> Answer: Google
>
>

Updated job classifications and job descriptions were created in accordance with the new definition of Production Control responsibilities and the upcoming reorganization. Pay grades were assigned. The reorganization was getting closer.

You may recall the description of Production Control's physical arrangement from the beginning of this chapter. Well, two unexpected events occurred which turned Production Control into the unit's show place. First, the Call Center that had occupied space adjacent to Production Control moved to a new location, and the department was able to take over that space, nearly doubling its area. Then, the unit's facilities department decided to experiment with a new office furniture system, and because Production Control was the shabbiest department in the unit, it was selected to be the guinea pig for the first experiment.

A designer from the furniture's manufacturer worked closely with the department, laying out Production Control's needs for the present and for after the reorganization. The new, improved Production Control area was sleek and beautiful and included cubicles for supervisors and systems analysts, a conference area, plenty of storage space, ample work stations, and an office for Dana. The reconfigured space made performing all aspects of daily work easier for everyone.

It also brought an enormous infusion of pride into the department. Pride and excitement had been building throughout the transformation as all staff members were actively involved in the projects that brought the changes about, but there was something especially powerful about having beautiful surroundings after years of working amidst broken, mismatched furniture. In response, the entire staff met privately and adopted a dress code for the department.

The last huge project standing in the way of Production Control's complete transformation was tackling the programming areas. Here are a few of the changes that resulted:

Whereas programmers had become accustomed to making changes to production jobs whenever and however they pleased without notifying anyone, now, as Production Control put jobs on the automated scheduler, they moved those jobs into a protected area. All changes from that point on had to be formally requested, and Production Control made the changes.

In addition, while Production Control had traditionally accepted jobs without run documentation, now department staff designed a new format for run documentation and also created an abbreviated online version for the programmers' convenience. Production Control then stopped accepting jobs without documentation.

Production Control also had been expected to add jobs to the production schedule at any time of day at anyone's request. The department now set up a formal job schedule request system that required notification during first shift for any jobs to be run that night, along with the signature of a programming manager.

As with all the other innovations Production Control proposed, each of these changes had to be negotiated with the programming managers before Production Control was permitted to act on them.

The final piece of the transformation was set in motion when Dana and his systems analysts asked to sit on the data center standards committee, a group of programming and data center managers charged with completing the previously abandoned task of writing a standards manual. When the committee reached the sections that involved Production Control, the department team was ready with numerous suggestions (and justifications) for standards covering documentation, operational considerations, problem resolution, and job verification and distribution. Everything that Production Control believed would contribute to standardization, security, and error-free processing was incorporated into the standards manual.

The formal reorganization of Production Control was announced a few weeks later. After two and a half years of consistent effort, the department had indeed been transformed—from a chaotic, dysfunctional, snarling mess to a department inspired by its commitment to Aliass Publishing's subscribers, and happily engaged in ". . . scheduling, submitting, and overseeing successful completion of all batch production jobs with continuously improving accuracy, smoothness, and efficiency." That short statement of purpose guided Production Control staff members as they reenvisioned and reconstructed everything about their department.

Surprisingly, the transformation of Production Control also affected other areas in the subscription fulfillment unit. For example:

The Production Control problem reporting system was duplicated and used by product and programming areas as well as the data center. It became the model for the entire subscription fulfillment unit.

In addition, the standards that Production Control requested for work coming into the department had the effect of standardizing procedures in the programming areas as well. This led to structural consistency among development projects and gave programming managers practical criteria for evaluating their programmers' performance.

Finally, following Production Control's example, other areas also began focusing on automating manual processes. This resulted in greater time efficiency and fewer processing errors across the subscription unit.

The story of Aliass Publishing illustrates that organizational units have the freedom to create their own statements of purpose, whether because there is no purpose communicated by the larger organization, or to support the larger organization's purpose. Either way, the unit can use its statement of purpose to guide its structure, direction, activities, and priorities—to its own benefit, and in all likelihood, to the benefit of the larger organization.

Such is the power of an applied purpose.

To Recap

◆ Our second example of applying purpose to organizational management involves a nonprofit publisher with no clear organizational purpose.

◆ A department within the organization formulated its own purpose, then used that purpose to completely redesign itself.

◆ Changes created within a small department can generate improvements throughout an entire organization.

Chapter Five

Applying Organizational Purpose, Part Three

IN THIS CHAPTER

····→ Which comes first, the organization or the purpose?

····→ How, specifically, can purpose be used to effectively manage an organization?

····→ How can we ensure that our purposes remain relevant over time?

Back when she was new to the workforce and lacking educational credentials, Alex took a job with an employment agency as a placement specialist. She was extremely excited because she had just been through a discouraging, confidence-battering job search herself, and thought how wonderful it would have been to have had a guide through the process: someone who could have told her about job openings, scheduled interviews for her, raved about her talent and work ethic to prospective employers in ways she couldn't do herself without sounding like a braggart, and negotiated her salary without awkwardness or apology. Alex couldn't wait to start making it easier for other job seekers to find suitable, satisfying work.

Once on the job, Alex was put to work phoning companies that she selected at random from the phone book and asking them if they had any employment openings. If they did, she was to persuade them to (a) give her the details of the position and (b) agree to pay a fee to Alex's employment agency if the agency filled their opening.

Alex quickly learned that the employment agency was run entirely on numbers: each placement specialist had a quota for number of job orders taken and placements made per month; and each placement specialist was expected to send job seekers out on interviews within twenty-four hours of their registering at the agency, whether or not the interview was for a job matching their skills and interests. As Alex's supervisor put it: "If we send them out immediately they'll think we're really working for them."

There was no personal involvement or attentiveness invested by the agency in discovering or working toward the best interests of either their job seekers or prospective employers.

Alex left the employment agency after a few months.

Many years and a full career later, Alex decided to revisit the whole notion of employment services. Job seekers' need for someone to guide, instruct, and represent them through the employment process clearly existed for thousands of job seekers, just as it had for Alex when she was inexperienced, uncredentialed, and looking for work. Alex was also very aware of how inadequately prepared hiring employers generally were to define their needs, screen their candidates, construct interviews, and hire the right people. She conceived of an organization that could make the employment process easier and the outcomes more satisfying for both seekers and employers, and so Aliass Employment was born.

> ### What's Wrong with This Purpose Statement?
>
> *To solve unsolved problems innovatively.*
>
> Answer: Math problems? Economic problems? Relationship problems? This statement doesn't give enough information for us to discern its Why or What or How.
>
> **food for thought**

Realizing that she would need help with her experiment, Alex approached four colleague-friends with her idea and invited all of them to join her in creating a new, different kind of organization. After much discussion— between the five of them, in smaller groups, and one on one—they all enthusiastically accepted Alex's invitation, and they agreed to open the new venture the following year.

During that year, they met frequently so that Alex could teach her partners everything they needed to know about the employment process from both job seeker and employer perspectives, including overviews, specific components, and actual skills.

They also used the year to lay out their plans for the new organization.

Statement of Purpose and the Plan

The partners began by creating Aliass Employment's statement of purpose:

> *Aliass Employment envisions a world in which all employed people are engaged in work that uses their talents well, and offers them challenge, opportunities, and satisfaction. To that end, we teach job seekers the skills they need to proficiently plan and conduct their employment searches; we teach hiring employers how to competently, responsibly conduct their new employee searches; we put job seekers and hiring employers together; and we coach both sides to successful placements.*

The team believed that challenging, satisfying employment would change life in a positive way for both employees and their employers. And, they reasoned, since millions of people spend tens of millions of hours at work each year, if they could bring to all employment and employee seekers an understanding of how the employment process can work to everyone's advantage, they could change the world. They decided to go big with Aliass Employment.

They then reviewed the activities they intended to perform in service of their vision and separated them according to whether they were revenue generating or non-revenue-generating.

Putting job seekers and hiring employers together (job placement) and providing coaching/consulting to prospective employers to ensure successful hires and turnover prevention would both produce revenue. Teaching employers how to competently, responsibly conduct their new employee searches had some potential for generating income, whereas teaching job seekers the skills necessary to proficiently plan and conduct their employment searches would bring in little to no revenue.

They decided to focus on their revenue generating activities first, and, once that portion of the business was profitable, they would use a substantial share of the profits to support their various employment training activities. They created a master calendar which laid out goals, action plans, and assignments by time frames. All goals and action plans on the calendar directly supported the statement of purpose.

Organizational Purpose and Staffing

Within the first year, they intended to have a staff of fifteen. Staff members were hired initially as part-timers, persuaded to accept very small salaries in exchange for enormous future growth potential (plus the thrill of helping change the world), and then trained to recruit job seekers. The founders were clear about their requirements for Aliass Employment part-time staff: "Must quickly and effortlessly establish connections and trust with diverse others; must have no previous recruiting/placement experience whatsoever; and, a nontraditional work history is preferred."

Once part-time recruiters were trained, competent, and productive, they began learning the placement end of employment. Compensation evolved into a base plus commission structure so that staff members had ultimate control over their earnings, and Aliass Employment could keep a tight rein on its costs. Hours were expanded for staff members who wanted to work full time, and more part-timers were added. As Aliass Employment grew, it needed additional staff to handle financial matters, IT, social media/blogging, marketing, and administrative support. The firm's first choice always was to transfer or promote a recruiter, but occasionally it would have to hire from the outside. All staff members, no matter the job for which they were hired, underwent training in recruiting and placement first; the founders were convinced that if staff members in support areas thoroughly understood the revenue generating work of Aliass Employment, they would perform more effectively and be seen by the revenue generators as team members rather than outsiders. Ultimately, all staff attended the workshops designed for job seekers and hiring employers as well, and anyone who was interested in teaching was welcome to sign up for facilitator training.

Aliass Employment envisioned a world where all employed people would be engaged in work that used their talents well and offered them challenge, opportunities, and satisfaction. Naturally, Aliass Employment expected to be such a place itself.

The organization selected staff, across job responsibilities, who were flexible, smart, highly competent, well educated (not necessarily credentialed), and hungry for more experience, new opportunities, new skills, *more*. Their ability to quickly establish rapport with employers, job seekers, or anyone, was outstanding, their attention was clearly focused, and their care was genuine. They were able to think independently, speak articulately, and they brought equal parts intensity and playfulness to the workplace. They were far more interested in facilitating someone else's success than in pointing out their own. And they loved Aliass Employment's dynamic work environment.

> ## Whose Organizational Purpose Is This?
>
> *We believe, very simply, that it is the actions of individuals working together that build strong communities . . . and that business has an obligation to support those actions in the communities it serves.*
>
> Answer: Bank of America

Within a year, the staff had grown to seventeen; by the end of the second year there were twenty-eight employees and by the beginning of the fourth year, there were forty-two. Aliass Employment was continually growing, but the growth was deliberate, structured, and therefore minimally disruptive. One of the founders likened it to "new guests arriving at the party."

Organizational Purpose and Structure/Physical Arrangement

Aliass Employment's founders carefully considered how to structure their organization so that it would complement their purpose and provide the workplace experiences they wanted for themselves and for their staff members. They laid out their plan before they hired any additional staff, and then simply worked with the framework they had devised, anticipating that it would support their organizational purpose. As they grew, Aliass Employment monitored whether its structure was facilitating or obstructing workflow, communication, and project development and, with staff participation, made adjustments where necessary. These adjustments were few and minor, evidence of their plan's effectiveness.

Setting up a highly centralized or hierarchical structure—with multiple layers of management, limited flexibility, and very little employee involvement in information sharing or decision making—would have been totally inappropriate for Aliass Employment, since the founders valued organization-wide collaboration and their staff members were competent, independent thinkers and talkers.

Similarly, they rejected a functional approach to structuring Aliass Employment because they had all noticed that dividing staff by the tasks they performed tended to encourage competition and discourage cooperation between units, teams, and individuals in other organizations with which they were familiar. While this may have been ideal in some organizations, since Aliass Employment favored a collaborative approach, any structural configuration that stimulated internal competition was unappealing. Functional approaches also, unintentionally, tend to stress the differences between units rather than their common objective: to contribute to the purpose of the larger organization. And Aliass Employment was completely committed to fulfilling its organizational purpose.

Having found the two most common mainstream structures incompatible with their organizational purpose, the partners decided to develop their own custom setup, one that would enable, encourage, support, and contribute to the experiences of good fit, collaboration, opportunity, and satisfaction that they wanted for everyone affiliated with Aliass Employment.

First, they considered reporting relationships. They had deliberately selected and hired staff members who were self-directing. As a consequence, formally appointing a group of supervisors seemed unnecessary. Instead, they developed a team approach, based around projects or hiring-employer clients. In most cases, whoever brought in the client or initiated the project became the team leader, but, for variety, sometimes team leaders were selected by lottery or because someone built a strong case for leading a particular team, and the others agreed. Team leaders chose their team members through personal invitation and/ or staff volunteering. It was not unusual for team members to be involved with several teams at any given time. Team leaders, team members, and team roles all rotated among staff members as projects were completed, or a hiring employer's needs changed or were met. These rotations gave everyone opportunities to (a) eventually work with everyone else and (b) acquire new skills in a relatively risk-free environment, since there were experts on each team to teach, support, and ensure excellence for the client or project. The five founders participated on teams with everyone else.

Support staff members were encouraged to create small teams crossing areas of expertise. These teams worked together part time on projects that they jointly conceived. Examples include: developing new services or products to advance Aliass Employment's purpose; upgrading current ones; summarizing research on the latest trends and thought in employment for dissemination to everyone else; and creating systems/procedures to make doing Aliass Employment's work easier and more effective.

Now that Aliass Employment had teams set up, decision making was the next logical topic for the partners to take on. They settled on a general procedure that consisted of preassignment sit-downs with the project or client team and one of the partners. At these meetings they discussed the general direction and then specific components of the work the team would be doing. The team then made whatever decisions needed to be made, using whatever process they selected to ensure that their decisions supported Aliass Employment's organizational purpose.

Staff members in non-employment-related roles (IT, finance, administrative support, etc.) generally worked in pairs; the groups were empowered to make all decisions relating to their areas, again guided by purpose and values.

There was almost no turnover among Aliass Employment staff members. The organization had been designed to offer staff members the freedom to pursue their professional interests by experimenting with different roles and learning new skills. Those who preferred more structure could create it for themselves, or ask for assistance. Aliass Employment filled its space with nontraditional, curious, caring people for whom the environment and work chosen by the founders was itself motivating and fulfilling.

Finally, the founders planned Aliass Employment's physical arrangement and layout. They left the particulars to an architect and a designer, but they made it clear that, because of the structure they had created, they needed maximum flexibility in their physical environment.

The design team gave them a combination of light, open space where multiple people could work simultaneously—together, individually, or in smaller groups—and individual office spaces of varying sizes, to accommodate staff members who needed quiet for reading, thinking, planning, or private meetings. There was a library, a kitchen/break room, and a storage room with lockers for staff members' personal belongings. Because of the fluidity of Aliass Employment's teams, all equipment and furniture was designed to be portable, and the work stations weren't assigned. The arrangement was circular, with storage components topped by computer screens in the center, the open space with work stations radiating outward and the private offices around the perimeter.

The arrangement worked very well for the first couple of years, but as Aliass Employment approached thirty-five employees, the teams and partners jointly decided to assign work stations. The arrangement that had supported flexibility at twenty employees was cumbersome and distracting at thirty-five. Work stations were assigned.

Organizational Purpose and Work Processes

While Aliass Employment was new and all attention was directed toward building revenue through job placement and coaching/consulting to employers, the five partners spent four days per week developing relationships with employer clients, working with job seekers, making placements, and providing follow-up services to ensure smooth transitions for both employers and their new employees. They spent the fifth day each week collaborating in various combinations on developing their training programs for job seekers and hiring employers.

As the organization began to grow, the founders invited all new staff members to allocate up to 20 percent of their scheduled hours toward working on projects of their choosing, consistent with the purpose and work of Aliass Employment, but apart from their daily assignments. They were free to work in teams or on their own.

Whose Organizational Purpose Is This?

To constantly improve what is essential to human progress by mastering science and technology.

Answer: The Dow Chemical Company

This program provided staff members with the growth, challenge, and satisfaction envisioned in Aliass Employment's purpose statement, and it also advanced the organization's development of workshops for job seekers and hiring employers.

Initially, Aliass Employment worked directly with its clients, meeting in person with hiring employers and job seekers, and eventually holding stand-up workshops for both groups. The special projects program gave birth to experiments in alternate methods of delivering Aliass Employment's trainings. This ultimately made Aliass Employment's approach and practical techniques accessible to more job seekers and employers, in more organizations, in more cities, in more . . . resulting in more people learning how to conduct their employment searches with confidence, skill, and effectiveness. Which brought Aliass Employment more opportunities to change the world.

Organizational Purpose and Performance

In my experience, one of the biggest challenges an organization faces is understanding which of the many activities it performs and relationships it conducts are the ones that are critical to its success. It's important to know this, because then those activities and relationships can be measured, and the measures will reveal how the organization is performing. Knowing where things stand provides the foundation for goal setting or course correction.

Sadly, many organizations are seduced by the factors that are easiest to measure, and they end up with a distorted or incomplete picture of their performance because they've measured the wrong things.

If we were Aliass Employment, how would we avoid this trap? We'd rely on our purpose for direction, which is what Aliass Employment did. Let's review the setup: Aliass Employment's ultimate goal was to bring the knowledge and skills needed to conduct effective, responsible, successful job/employee searches to job seekers and hiring employers alike. Most of the formal training would be non-revenue-generating, so Aliass Employment set up a revenue generating recruiting and placement group to pay its staff and fund its educational activities.

In this example, the cleanest, easiest performance indicators to measure would be monthly numbers of job orders taken, interviews scheduled, job seekers in the applicant pool, placements made, dollars billed and received, job seekers trained, hiring employers trained, and on and on. This is interesting information, but it won't show how Aliass Employment is performing with respect to its underlying reasons for doing recruiting, placement, and training.

Here are some of the things Aliass Employment decided to measure, and why:

◆ Percentage of active job seekers who became employed each month. This indicated knowledge/understanding of job search techniques.

◆ Percentage of newly employed seekers who were still on the job after ninety days. This indicated good fit.

◆ Percentage of placed seekers who left their jobs within ninety days. This indicated the need to explore what happened, how it might have been avoided, what to do differently next time.

◆ Number and dollar amounts of refunds paid each month. Aliass Employment's policies included refunds of placement fees if the employee/employer relationship ended within the first ninety days of employment (100 percent during the first thirty days, 65 percent for the next thirty days, and 35 percent for the final thirty days). It was important to understand the financial costs of unsuccessful placements, too.

What's Wrong with This Purpose Statement?

The purpose of IJK is to earn money for its shareholders and increase the value of their investment. We will do that through growing the company, controlling assets, and properly structuring the balance sheet, thereby increasing EPS, cash flow, and return on invested capital.

Answer: Here we have a *What* and a *How*, but the absence of a *Why* explains this organization's single-minded focus on money.

food for thought

◆ Recently employed job seekers' satisfaction with their new jobs. Job satisfaction for employees was at the core of Aliass Employment's purpose.

◆ Hiring employers' satisfaction with their new employees. This demonstrated good fit, and employer satisfaction was also at the core of Aliass Employment's purpose.

You get the idea. Collecting numbers is always easy; measuring intangibles such as satisfaction, confidence, learning, and others, is much more difficult. Happily, there are now scads of instruments available that measure pretty much anything. And organizations can always ask their clients/customers/users directly about their experiences and opinions. The point is: don't give up trying to measure the right things because it seems impossible. It isn't, any more.

We have just seen how Aliass Employment began planning and designing all facets of its organization a year before it officially opened, which is highly unusual. Nevertheless, I think it's the ideal scenario because planning ahead provided these founding partners with the time and space to choose deliberately how they would link every aspect of organizational operation to their larger purpose. As a result, their structure, work processes, staffing, performance management, and everything else within Aliass Employment was set up in accordance with its purpose, and, once established, all those functions, in turn, supported its purpose.

The ease and stability that come from consistently applying the same purpose, principles, and values to the different facets of an organization make managing that organization almost effortless. Setting up an organization based on a purpose beyond being profitable also creates an environment where staff members can flourish.

In the case of Aliass Employment, opportunities for making decisions combined with fluid roles, assignments, and team memberships maximized the potential for staff members to learn, grow, achieve, and collaborate. Time in the office with the freedom to create projects, read, or contemplate provided opportunities for inspiration, challenge, excitement, and fun.

Finally, as we saw in the grocery stores example from **Chapter Two**, when an organization is directed by its purpose, it automatically draws clients or customers who resonate with the way it conducts itself, which, simply, is its *Why*, its *What*, and its *How* in action. It's a beautiful thing.

We've come to our final chapter. This is where we'll discuss how you can take everything we've talked about so far and begin experimenting with it yourself. Using organizational purpose to manage your own organization may sound daunting, but as we've seen in our examples, it's absolutely doable. The first step? Turn the page.

To Recap

◆ The organization featured in our third example is a not-only-for-profit employment training and placement firm.

◆ The founders planned for a year before launching their venture.

◆ When purpose is used to direct an organization's structure, work processes, staffing, performance management, and everything else, managing the organization becomes effortless.

Chapter Six

Bringing It Home

IN THIS CHAPTER

- ┅➔ What can we learn from the detailed examples?

- ┅➔ How can we apply the principles presented here to our organizations?

- ┅➔ How can we use our purposes to manage our organizations?

We've seen three very different organizations find their ways to an understanding of the importance of their organizations' statements of purpose, as both management tools and sources of inspiration.

Aliass Consulting opened its first branch office with a simple business plan: get clients, hire consultants, do large, complex, long-lasting projects. When things didn't unfold as Aliass Consulting's leaders expected, they abruptly changed the game plan, heedless of the impact this would have on their technical staff and, eventually, their clients and revenue. They saw the light, to an extent, and developed a philosophy that then guided their decision making in the areas of structure, work processes, and management. Soon after, they added a staff support program that guided their performance management, communication, and staffing policies.

I selected this example to illustrate that even when a statement of purpose is incomplete or arrives in phases, it can still be a powerful, effective ally in the managing of an organization.

The Aliass Publishing story shows us how a dysfunctional, chaotic, overwhelmed, victimized department was able to metamorphose into a slick, efficient, self-directing, respected department once it had a very clear purpose that was sincerely endorsed by all department members—who were then able to create the unity, inspiration, and direction required to drive the desperately needed changes.

This example teaches us that no matter how dire or seemingly hopeless our organizational circumstances may seem, they can be remedied when we have clarity about *Why* we exist, *What* we do to enliven that underlying purpose, and *How* we perform our activities so that our choices are consistent with our organizational values.

Our final illustration, Aliass Employment, presents the ideal scenario: an organization defines its purpose *before* it opens its doors. It sets up the framework for every aspect of its operation into the future, in accordance with its purpose. Then, since the organization has anticipated and planned for growth, there is no not knowing what to do with new staff members, no confusion, no chaos, no frustration, no dismay, no problem.

The big lesson for all of us is that there isn't just one way to use organizational purpose as a management tool. It's flexible and forgiving. So take your time and collaborate with the rest of your organization on a statement of purpose. Then work together to develop the process you'll use to take your organization where it has to be to fulfill its purpose.

Revising your organization so that everything it does will be guided by its purpose takes time and generally requires a substantial number of projects to be completed. When you're setting up your master schedule, make it a point to intersperse short-term projects among the long-term projects, so that there are perpetually projects being completed. On those occasions, throw a party in your organization, put up streamers and balloons, give everybody a kazoo, break out the sparkling cider, celebrate the teams who worked on the project and spend half an hour or so together, feeling the joy that comes from making progress. This will enable your staff to see that, even though the end is not yet in sight, the plans you've made together are coming to fruition. Besides, how fun!

 practical tip

You can do this. And it can be exciting beyond your craziest imagining. Here's some final advice.

The Foundation

In order for any attempt at managing an organization through its purpose to succeed, there has to be trust: between managers and subordinates, between staff and boards of directors, between functional units, between shifts, and between individual staff members. Since organizational trust levels in general have been declining for some time, recognizing where your organization stands with respect to trust between its members is a good place to begin.

How can you know whether you have trust issues in your organization? They show up in behaviors or characteristics such as in the following partial list:

- withholding information
- playing politics
- micromanaging
- constant conflict
- empire building
- turf protection
- sabotage
- malicious obedience
- poor performance
- dysfunction
- low morale

If any of these seem even remotely familiar to you, you probably have trust problems in your organization. They must be repaired before you try to move forward with anything else. To try to implement any sort of lasting organizational change where trust is lacking is to invite complete failure. Guaranteed.

So let's suppose that you've discovered low trust levels somewhere in your organization. What's next? The most important thing you can do initially is activate your patience and be prepared for this trust building journey to set its own pace. Don't try to rush it; that will only engender new mistrust. Relax, smile, be confident that trust within your organization will be achieved eventually (it will) and focus on the things you can do to create a new atmosphere of trust. Such as:

Be open about what you're trying to do ("I feel a lack of trust within our organization, and I'd like to change that.")

Ask what others think, not because it's a technique but because you're actually interested. ("Here's what I'm thinking of doing to help build trust; what do you think?")

Listen uncritically to what they have to say. If they're reluctant to share what they think, accept it and move on. Try again another time.

If you want staff members to give you input or feedback, telling them that you value their opinions, your door is always open, and they can drop by any time, probably won't work; they won't be sure what kind of input you want, they'll feel awkward and they'll avoid the whole thing. Instead, ask for the specific feedback you need and they'll know how to respond.

practical tip

Be sure to follow through on your own commitments. Do what you say you'll do.

Let others in on whatever information you have about the organization that they don't have. I have never understood the need for secrets in organizations (with the exceptions of staff medical conditions and other private information about individuals); keeping staff members in the dark, in my experience, prevents them from contributing fully to the organization and leads them to feel left out and distrusted.

Treat others with trust. The best manager I ever had earned that rank with me because he always assumed that I would succeed and let me know it. Very powerful.

Be consistent. You can't be interested in someone's opinions one day and not have time the next, if you want to earn trust.

Accept that trust building will take time and effort. Keep at it, don't get discouraged, don't even think about giving up, and celebrate the subtle signs that will appear to let you know that things are beginning to change. The first changes will be fragile, so be gentle lest you chase them away. You will find, when you have triumphed, that it was completely worth the time, effort, and discomfort. Trust me.

Your Organizational Purpose

Congratulations! You have become an organization brimming with trust and good will. (See how easy and enjoyable that was?) That means it's time to talk organizational purpose with your organization.

The Preliminaries

But first, it's important to get a handle on precisely where things stand within your organization. Think about Aliass Publishing and how its entire department overhaul was sparked by learning what was really going on in Production Control.

My favorite technique for discovering where things actually stand in an organization involves two steps.

Step One: Hold brief meetings with everyone in your organization, one unit at a time. Try to do all these meetings on the same day to minimize rumors, false reports, or hurt feelings because some people were included in the first day's meetings and others weren't. (You know what I'm talking about.) Tell them simply that you've got some concerns about life and work in your organization, and that you'd like their opinions regarding what's working and what's not working.

Step Two: Ask specifically for their input regarding what they think your organization does well, what they think your organization doesn't do so well, and any suggestions they have for improving organizational performance and organizational life. Set up flip charts in groups of three in various locations throughout your organization, and invite staff members to enter their input on the appropriate charts. (Make sure there's enough space between the charts for some privacy; headings should be: What We Do Well; What We Don't Do Well; Suggestions.) Encourage them to check out all the flip charts to see what others have written, because someone else's comment might trigger another idea of theirs. Leave the charts up for several days; then ask for some volunteers to help collate the input and compile the three lists.

Getting Started

Once you've emailed the lists to everyone, it's time to get them together in an informal setting for an organization-wide meeting. The primary advantage to having everybody together is that it enables all organizational members to participate in the same event. The second advantage is the energy potential in the room. Wow.

Begin by thanking them for taking part in the flip chart exercise; then present a brief summary of all the input and suggestions. Invite their comments. Next, you could share your vision for the organization, or you could discuss your own assessment of what's working and what's not working, or you could suggest that in order to effectively address the things that aren't working so well in your organization, you need to clarify your organization's reason for existing, because: if you don't know *why* you're here—which is what informs *what* you do and *how* you do it—then how can you know what to do or how to do it?

You know your organization, so you will know how best to approach your meeting. I do suggest, however, that you structure it so that your folks feel free to ask questions, make comments and generally participate, and that you schedule time for a discussion of the theory and practice of organizational purpose. This is critical since an organization's purpose has to be known and endorsed by its members in order to do its magic.

> Do not solicit feedback or input from your staff members unless you are committed to doing something with the information you receive. Few actions erode trust more quickly or effectively than asking for feedback or input and then ignoring it.
>
>  practical tip

I'm going to assume that you've persuaded a majority of your organization's members that developing a statement of purpose is the right next step. So how do you do it?

Almost There . . .

You probably don't want to duplicate the mission statement committee fiascoes of the 1990s, so you'll need a different process for creating your statement of purpose.

In my view, it's important to include everyone in this process, and there are many ways to do that. Here are a couple of them:

You could focus on the *Why* by itself, and ask everyone to think about and then write an answer to the question: What is the reason for this organization's existence? Have a box with a slot in the top ready for their responses. When you and your volunteers go through them, you'll put the jokes aside and then group similar ones together. Present the options to the entire staff, and majority vote determines the selection. Since you're an ongoing operation, you most likely already have your *What*, but you could repeat the above process to clarify your *How*.

Or, you could ask organizational units to produce complete purpose statements, including the *Why*, the *What*, and the *How*. I picture a pep rally-type forum when the statements are ready, where each unit presents its purpose statement and explains its applicability to your organization. When all units have been heard, the organization votes.

Again, you know best what will work for your organization. Ideally, you'll all have some fun with this.

Extending and Applying Your Statement of Purpose

In a perfect world, once you have developed your organization's statement of purpose, each unit will want to create its own statement of purpose which will define how it fits in with and contributes to the larger organization's purpose.

Then (in a super perfect world), the individuals employed by your organization will want to create their own statements of purpose that explain how individuals fit in with and contribute to the purposes of their own work units and then to the larger organization.

Back in the real world, now that you have a statement of purpose to guide you, go back to your list of Things We Don't Do Well. Consider each item against your statement of purpose and ask whether your current procedure, policy, or whatever it is, is compatible with your purpose. My guess is that it won't be, so the next step is to figure out what sort of policy, procedure, or whatever it is *would* be compatible with your purpose. Do this with every item on the list, and your organizational overhaul plan will begin to take shape. You will be addressing the major complaints and inconveniences of your staff members, so they will be excited. Involve them in making plans for implementing the new, purpose-compatible policies and procedures, and they will be even more excited. Eventually, you will wonder if you still work in the same organization. The answer will be, "No." You now work in your organization transformed.

Understand that none of this developing statements of purpose and then reorienting organizations around them is quick or easy. However, it can definitely, assuredly, be done. And when you are in the company of colleagues who believe as you do that organizations can and should be places that inspire people to look forward to going to work, it can be an outright pleasure.

Best of luck to you, and have fun!

To Recap

◆ There is a whole assortment of ways to use organizational purpose as a management tool.

◆ Trust between organizational members and stakeholders is an essential part of any successful internal change.

◆ It will take time and effort, patience, and an unflagging sense of humor, but reworking your purpose so you can use it to drive everything you do is the greatest gift you can give yourself and everyone who works with you.

Index

A

Albuquerque Rescue Mission, 18–20, 22

C

Cub Foods, 17–18

G

Goodwill Industries, 11, 13–14

J

Jewel-Osco, 16–18

M

management, 12, 22, 24–25, 29–30, 33–34, 55, 63

  purpose as management tool, 7, 16, 63–64, 70

Metropolitan Homelessness Project, 19–20

Microsoft, 14–15

mission, 2–3, 5–7, 17, 20, 45

mission statement, 3–7, 15

  producing, 5

N

nonprofit organizations, 2, 23, 27

O

operations, 3, 9–10, 24, 27, 36, 42, 61, 64, 69

organizational management, 22, 24, 49

  effective, 2

  philosophies, 2

P

purpose

  components, 9, 11, 13, 15, 17, 19, 21, 24, 53, 57

  as management tool, 7, 16, 63–64, 70

  applied to organizational activities, 37

  applied to performance, 59

  applied to staffing, 54

  applied to structure/physical arrangement, 55

  applied to work processes, 58

  statement of, 10, 12

purpose statement, 10, 12
  applying to your organization, 63,
    65, 67, 69

S

Starbucks, 15, 42
statement of purpose, 10, 12
Sunset Foods, 16–18

V

values, 3, 5–7, 12–14, 17–18, 20, 57,
    60–61, 64, 66
values statement, 6, 12, 15
  Microsoft, 14–15
vision, 3, 5, 7, 29, 53, 68
vision statements, 5–6

If you enjoyed this book, you'll want to pick up the other books in the CharityChannel Press **In the Trenches**™ series.

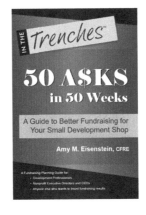

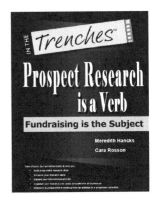

www.CharityChannel.com

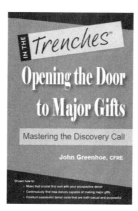

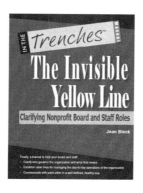

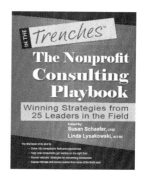

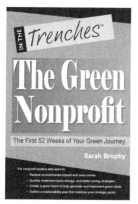

www.CharityChannel.com

CharityChannel

PRESS

And now introducing **For the GENIUS® Press,** an imprint that produces books on just about any topic that people want to learn. You don't have to be a genius to read a **GENIUS** book, but you'll sure be smarter once you do!

www.ForTheGENIUS.com

CPSIA information can be obtained at www.ICGtesting.com
Printed in the USA
LVOW01s2343160415

434916LV00011B/148/P